BUILD YOUR FIRST LAYOUT

Peter Vassallo

Kalmbach
Media

Kalmbach Media
21027 Crossroads Circle
Waukesha, Wisconsin 53186
www.KalmbachHobbyStore.com

Published in 2020
27 26 25 24 23   2 3 4 5 6

Manufactured in China

ISBN: 978-1-62700-777-1
EISBN: 978-162700-778-8

Editor: Eric White
Book Design: Kelly Katlaps

Library of Congress Control Number: 2019955648

Contents

Foreword 4

Chapter 1
The Northspur & Tiburon RR 6

Chapter 2
Benchwork and track 20

Chapter 3
Beginning scenery: making a mountain 30

Chapter 4
Scenery and structures: Part 1 38

Chapter 5
Scenery and structures: Part 2 54

Chapter 6
Scenery and structures: Part 3 70

Chapter 7
Finishing and operating 82

Foreword

If you're reading this book, you probably have a collection of model trains, or a recently purchased train set, and you're wondering what's next.

Searching online has shown you a dizzying array of options and some fantastic results. But how do you get from that stack of boxed rolling stock and track sections to something more?

That's what this book was written to show you. In seven chapters, and over a few months' time, you'll learn how to build benchwork, lay roadbed and track, create scenic contours, build structure kits, make a harbor scene, weather your rolling stock, and learn to operate trains in a reasonably realistic, and more importantly, fun way.

Peter Vassallo has been published in *Model Railroader* magazine and is a strong proponent of compact layouts. He built this layout to fit into his one-bedroom apartment, so you know it's not going to take up a lot of space.

This compact size means the project is also something that can be completed in a reasonable amount of time without a huge outlay of money.

Peter's benchwork is the tried-and-true open-grid method. He used a power miter saw and electric drill to cut and assemble the frame pieces, but with care and patience, the same work can be done with hand tools or simpler power tools.

His scenery base is carved extruded-foam insulation board, available at most building stores in a variety of thicknesses, and sometimes in easy-to-handle and transport 2 x 2-foot "project board" form.

Peter also shares his tips for building laser-cut wood structures and how to finish them to get satisfying results. Again, he uses readily available materials and methods aimed at the first-time layout builder.

So if you're ready to take your trains off the floor or dining room table and get them running through realistic scenes, this is a great place to start! Before you know it, you'll be delivering and picking up shipments at industries you've crafted yourself and simulating a slice of the business that has kept commerce and people moving for close to 200 years.

Have fun!
—Eric White

A small layout doesn't have to be boring. Peter Vassallo used readily available kits and materials to build a model railroad that will let a beginner develop his skills or entertain a long-time modeler.

CHAPTER ONE

The Northspur & Tiburon RR

What size layout do you think you would need to model a railroad connecting five towns over a distance of 200-plus miles, all in HO scale? You're probably picturing a good-sized room if not an entire basement—however, with a little imagination, all this is possible in just 4 x 6 feet.

An eastbound Southern Pacific SW1500 crosses a girder bridge in the Noyo River Canyon, midway between Fort Bragg and Northspur.

The Northspur & Tiburon (or N&T for short) started as a personal challenge to design an ultra-small HO scale layout that would happily engage one to three operators. And by engage I mean offering both switching and mainline running.

Pure switching-type layouts are fine up to a point, but to me, nothing beats running a train along the main and switching cars along the way. I find it much more enjoyable, after spending time switching a location, to just run the train for a while before tackling another switching job—particularly when the cars picked up from one place are delivered to another. This kind of operation is what railroading is all about and what appeals most to me.

The N&T is based loosely on two California prototypes: the California Western and the Northwestern Pacific. The California Western, otherwise known as the Skunk Line, ran 40 miles west from Willits to Fort Bragg on the Pacific coast. The Union

Lumber Company operated this line, which featured numerous logging camps and mills, in the early 1900s. Excursion trains continue to run on the line.

The Northwestern Pacific ran 200 miles southeast from Willits to Tiburon, servicing many stops along the way, including Petaluma, which adjoined a harbor. The terminal point at Tiburon along the San Francisco Bay had a classification yard, engine facilities, and a ferry, which interchanged with the Atchison, Topeka & Santa Fe. Parts of the line continue in commuter service today.

I did not model the prototype features explicitly, but rather their atmosphere and spirit. For example, due to the limited space, I substituted a wharf at Tiburon in place of the ferry. I also did not worry too much

Prototype map of the Northspur and Tiburon, representing routes from Willits to Fort Bragg and Willits to Tiburon. *Illustration by Rick Johnson*

A boxcar awaits unloading on the pier at Tiburon while dock workers clear some space.

Workers at Northspur prepare to load flat cars using a McGiffert log loader. It's a tight squeeze for those flat cars!

about matching prototype structures; as long as the structure looked good, fit the space, and performed its function, I was happy. I subscribe to the quantum principle of modeling anyway: where any variation to a prototype exists in an alternate (my) universe. No one can prove otherwise.

I built the layout over the course of a year in the living room of my one-bedroom apartment. Space constraints required I keep the layout small; however, I prefer small layouts anyway. They are portable and require less resources compared to larger layouts—in terms of space, time, money and maintenance (the last is a particular issue with me)—and can still allow for enjoyable operations.

Artistically, they can be satisfying as well—worthy of staring at and taking in. Even if you have a larger basement-type layout, that doesn't preclude you from building a second, smaller one,

tucking it into your den or living room, having fun with it and showing it off to visitors. People love watching trains go round, particularly when they are traveling through finely crafted, detailed scenes.

The layout design is a basic oval with a passing track and five spurs representing each of five towns. The passing track may be used by any of the towns during switching maneuvers. I've provided a track plan, including a schematic version, and a list of the structures I used.

I used curved turnouts to establish the passing track at the end of the layout. I required especially sharp radius turnouts and found that Peco offered the best choice. The company's Setrack turnouts have an effective outer radius of 19⅞" and an inner radius of 17¼". They are only available in code 100, however, so I used code 100 track for the main loop, harbor spurs and the

Brett's brewery and King's boathouse are the highlights of Petaluma.

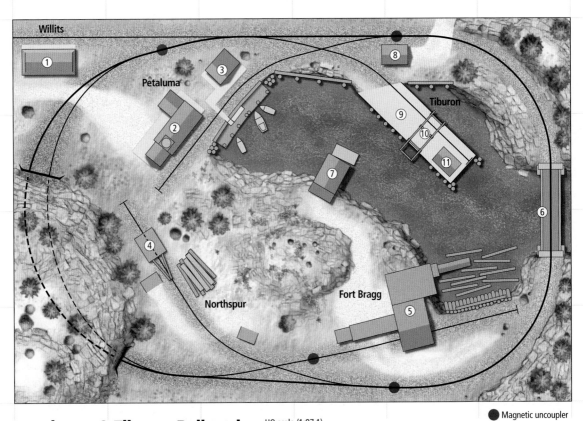

Willits

Petaluma

Tiburon

Northspur

Fort Bragg

● Magnetic uncoupler

Northspur & Tiburon Railroad

HO scale (1:87.1)
Layout size: 6 x 4 feet
Scale of plan: 1" = 1'-0", 12" grid
Illustration by Rick Johnson

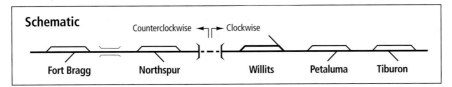

Schematic

Counterclockwise ← ⌐⌐ → Clockwise

Fort Bragg   Northspur   Willits   Petaluma   Tiburon

Structure list

Number	Structure	Model
1	Station	AMB Northern Pacific Class C Depot
2	Brewery	Campbell Bret's Brewery
3	Boathouse	AMB Grand Ave. Yard Office with a scratchbuilt deck and dock
4	Log loader	Rio Grande Models McGiffert Loader
5	Sawmill-Lumberyard	Campbell Saez Sash & Door with a scratchbuilt sawmill, jack-slip and log dump
6	Bridge	Central Valley 72-foot plate girder bridge No. 1903
7	Oyster house	Fos Scale Hooper's Oysters
8	Office tower	AMB Railroad Yard Office, No. 709
9	Pier	Scratchbuilt
10	Crane	Campbell Quincy Traveling Crane
11	Shed	Campbell Quincy Shed
Campbell Scale Models: campbellscalemodels.com		
American Model Builders (AMB): laserkit.com		
Rio Grande Models: riograndemodels.com		
Central Valley Model Works: cvmw.com		
Fos Scale Models: fosscalemodels.com		

Left: This schematic view of the layout shows the order of the towns as operators arrive at the given switch. Trains start in Willits, then head either westbound (counterclockwise) a few laps to Northspur and Fort Bragg, or south (clockwise) taking a few laps to get to Petaluma and Tiburon. To extend operations, I take a lap or two between switching moves. The passing siding is then convenient for all of the towns. *Illustration by Rick Johnson*

Logs are unloaded at the Fort Bragg sawmill, where personnel work to tip a pesky log into the pond for transfer into the mill. The spur accepts loaded flat cars as well as empty boxcars and hoppers for eventual loading with cut lumber and wood chips.

rest of the turnouts. Code 100 refers to the height of the rail in hundredths of an inch. Code 100 rail is .100 inches tall. I used smaller code 83 track for the logging spurs. This rail is .083 inches tall.

Trains running counterclockwise along the loop represent westbound trains, whereas trains running clockwise represent trains traveling south. From Willits, a train can proceed westbound a few laps, switch Northspur, continue west a few laps more, switch Fort Bragg, then return to Willits. Similar operations can occur for trains running south: from Willits to Petaluma to Tiburon, then back.

Note that one half of the layout represents the route from Willits to Fort Bragg and the other half, Willits to Tiburon. This allows operators to conveniently attend to their trains from either side of the layout. An engineer/conductor pair works especially well; the conductor issues switching orders, helps uncouple and throws turnouts from the near side, while the engineer runs the train from the far side. For variety, the two can switch duties between the Fort Bragg and Tiburon turns. The two operating positions also offer different views of the scenery and structures, enhancing the visual aspects of the layout.

The crossing tracks for the spurs are an artifact of the layout and should not be considered "there" when switching any given spur. The crossovers simply allow the spurs to separate from each other so more space is available. In this way, the towns are physically separated so you can focus on them one at a time while switching cars. The track arrangement also provides both facing and trailing moves during switching, spicing up operations.

Other operational schemes are possible if you don't want to model the five towns as described here. You can set up a scheme where the station is at one end of the line and the four towns are in sequence along

Southern Pacific No. 2476 with a short freight in tow heads north past the tower and office at Tiburon.

FRESH
OYSTERS

This overall view of the layout shows
Tiburon and its wharf at bottom center,
then, heading clockwise, is Fort Bragg
and the sawmill, Northspur and its
log loader next to the mountain, then
Petaluma on the water and Willits with
its depot back in the corner.

a single main line. Or the station can actually represent two "stations" book-ending the main line with four towns between them. You could also simplify the track plan by omitting the passing track; in that case, westbound trains leaving the station (counterclockwise on the loop) would switch the two towns with trailing spurs and enter the second station farther down the line. A new eastbound train (assembled by hand on the station track) would then return clockwise and switch the remaining two spurs.

The N&T can be built by an absolute newcomer to the hobby or by someone with many years of experience. The design is basic, yet allows for high levels of modeling and scenic treatment. In terms of operation, it is also surprisingly sophisticated. I imagine there are plenty of enthusiasts out there who are putting off building a layout due to lack of space, time or funds, or a perception that a lot of specialized equipment and skill is required.

I think the N&T would be perfect for them—it can be built simply, practically anywhere and at relatively low cost; the most expensive items are the structures and trains, which can be incorporated over time as the budget allows. Whether you decide to build it or not, I hope you will enjoy my presentation and thoughts on how I built the layout and learn something along the way that you can use.

Number 2476 waits at Willits for the southbound transfer to arrive. The transfer will leave cars on the station track destined for points farther south; No. 2476 will take it from there.

CHAPTER TWO

Benchwork and track

An office worker enjoys the switching activity on the Tiburon pier from the balcony of the nearby tower. Before we can build scenes like this, we have to build the benchwork and track.

The beginning of a project is always exciting, but bear in mind there will be challenges ahead. Speaking for myself, although I've built layouts before, I still encountered many issues this

time, some of my own making. (It's a fact of life that not everything can be anticipated or executed correctly. Also, patience is not my strong suit). And if I build another layout next year, I would undoubtedly have a whole new set of problems to deal with. That's just part of model railroading—you'd better be resourceful and determined or else you'll never make it.

I also have a tendency to dream big and get disappointed when the reality falls short. I have to keep pushing and get past these moments, deal with them as best I can, and perhaps come to appreciate the new reality. Again, this is part of the process. Also: while I enjoy layout design and building to plan, I try to remain open to creative impulses as I go. These impulses often lead to better, more interesting results than originally conceived. Don't be afraid to experiment.

The humble beginnings of the N&T: This is all of the benchwork material ready to go.

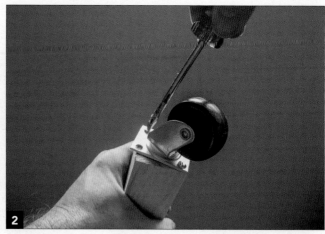

A simple method for attaching the casters to legs, using two screws on the diagonal.

Living in an apartment, I used this convenient method for drilling pilot holes: two TV trays as supports and a trash can to catch sawdust.

The assembled frame resting on my living room floor.

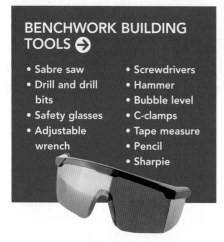
Okay, enough talk. Let's get started. I've provided lists of the tools I used. Most of these are basic tools you probably already have. While not absolutely necessary, a Dremel motor tool makes trackwork much easier to cut and fit and is also useful down the road when constructing models. It's a good hobby investment.

Benchwork construction

I purchased all the wood from my local big box home center (two trips). I spent some time looking through the pine boards to select the straightest ones. The boards were 6 or 8 feet long, and fit comfortably inside my compact Toyota RAV4 SUV. Later, I took these pieces to a friend's house so I could use his table saw and cut them to the proper sizes. I wanted the cuts to be clean and straight. For the plywood, I had 2 feet trimmed off the end of a 4 x 8-foot piece at the home center. I was then able to squeeze the plywood into my car and carry it (with some difficulty) into my apartment. I purchased the Homasote at a nearby lumberyard and had them cut a 4 x 8-foot piece in half for me.

Once all the pieces were cut and ready to go, I cleared out a section of my apartment and began assembly, **1**. Since I wanted some mobility to the layout, I attached inexpensive casters to the ends of the leg pieces. I cocked the casters so that two small corner screws could fasten them while still keeping the casters centered, **2**. Next, I drilled ⅛-inch diameter pilot holes into the frame side boards; this prevents splitting the wood when using drywall screws to attach the cross joists. I found a pair of TV dinner stands useful for holding the wood while

5

This simple method for attaching the legs to the frame uses two bolts, washers, and nuts arranged orthogonally.

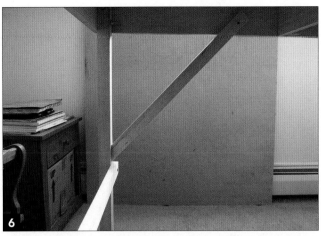

6

This detail view shows the leg supports. I didn't use any glue on these connections so the legs could be removed in the future, if necessary.

7

The frame and leg assembly stands complete and ready for the top surface.

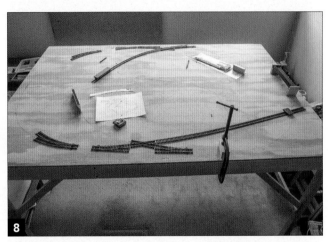

8

I placed the plywood on the frame and started laying out the track. Turnouts, crossovers, and selected spur tracks were positioned first, then I marked their locations with pencil lines. I have also positioned the bridge.

drilling, with a bag placed underneath to catch the shavings, **3**. I used these TV stands often during construction of the layout, as you will see.

After the pilot holes were drilled in the side pieces, I positioned them with the cross joists on the floor, applied wood glue to the joints, and screwed each joist to the side boards using two screws at each joint, **4**. Newspaper under the wood caught any excess glue. I wiped away the excess glue on the joint using a damp rag. The legs were added next, using two ¼-inch bolts orthogonally positioned at each joint, **5**. I attached leg braces using drywall screws. The bolts and screws can be removed in the future if I want to transport the layout. Lastly, I glued some wood blocks into the corners of

the interior joints to help strengthen and complete the frame, **7**.

At this point, I lifted the plywood onto the frame. The plywood had some warp to it, so I clamped and screwed it down to the frame to level it out. I then began positioning the turnouts and track, **8**. To help, I printed out a track plan, scaled so that 1 inch on the plan corresponded to 10 inches on the layout. This allowed me to easily locate various track components and see how everything looked. I penciled in the basic shapes, curves and turnouts, and positioned the bridge at one end of the layout. I also cut out a newspaper template of the wharf and placed it in its proper location.

After reviewing the arrangement several times, I drew the shape of the

TRACK LAYING TOOLS →

- Utility knife
- Needle-nose pliers
- Motor tool with a cut-off wheel and grinding wheel
- Soldering iron and solder
- Thumbtacks
- String and eyebolt

harbor using a black marker, **9**. Except for locations where retaining walls would be used, I added 2 inches from the water line to where I drew the harbor line to allow for the banks. I used a sabre saw to cut out the harbor. I also cuts notches in the joists below to accommodate the harbor floor.

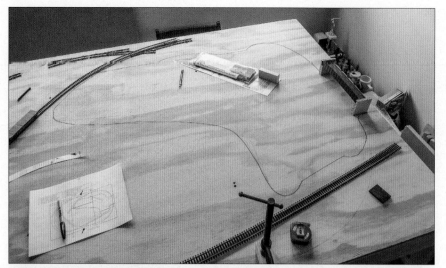

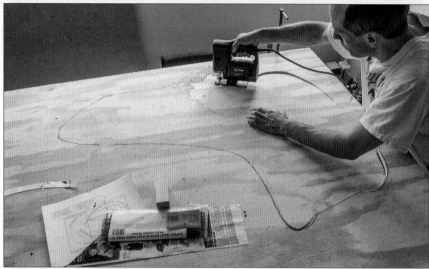

9

Top: I traced the harbor outline using a black marker. Center: I used a sabre saw to cut out harbor. Bottom: I cut notches in the joists below the harbor to recess the harbor surface below track level.

These notches were 2 inches deep. I added additional cross joists below the harbor for extra support.

I later decided to use ⅛-inch thick tempered hardboard (sold under the Masonite brand name, among others) for the harbor bottom rather than plywood. This meant I had to glue ⅜-inch-thick spacer strips to the benchwork supporting the harbor to raise it to the correct height. If you plan on using the same method to model water, you should cut 1⅝-inch notches in the benchwork rather than 2 inches.

After the notches and additional cross joists were added, I glued and screwed the plywood down to the frame, **10**. I staged the plywood by using small blocks at the frame corners to hold the plywood above the frame. I then applied wood glue to the top of the frame, removed the spacer blocks, then screwed the plywood down. I did not attach the harbor surface to the frame just yet.

Track, up-front thoughts

Before starting to lay track, there were a few decisions I needed to make. For one, I had to decide what uncoupling method to use on the layout, manual or magnetic. Many folks nowadays prefer the manual method, using bamboo skewers or a similar tool to uncouple. With this approach, you avoid the complexity of installing magnets and you can uncouple anywhere.

However, using the skewer can be difficult; speaking for myself, I cannot seem to get the knack and spend an inordinate amount of time twisting (and cursing) before the cars finally separate. I've had better experience with magnets, so that's what I'm using.

The question then becomes whether to use permanent magnets or electro-magnets. The main argument against permanent magnets is inadvertent uncoupling when trains pass by. Again, in my experience this rarely occurs if sufficient tension is maintained in the couplers. The tension can be increased by increasing the rolling resistance in the freight car wheels. Since for this layout the trains must be short, and there are no grades, the increased rolling resistance is not an issue with respect to locomotive capacity.

A feature of magnetic uncoupling is that by using delayed action, you can push cars back and leave them at any location behind the magnet, thus minimizing the number of magnets required. For this layout, I used four magnets to enable switching of all spurs. Note that all uncoupling actions will require some backward movement of the locomotive to position cars.

If you want the ability to easily remove the magnets, I suggest cutting out the plywood base below each magnet, allowing access from below. I believe if you are careful installing the magnets, you won't need to access them, so I simply secured them in place and covered them. If worse came to worst, I could always cut out the scenery around the magnets to access them. I made sure not to glue the foam down immediately next to the magnets to allow easy extraction if necessary.

As with uncoupling, you'll need to decide whether you want to actuate your turnouts trackside or remotely. Here I decided to stick with the basic, manual method that, in the case of Peco turnouts, is particularly easy since the locking mechanism is built right into the turnout and does not require an additional switch stand. This simplifies the installation and does not unduly hinder operations—actually, if a conductor is used during operations, manual switching of turnouts can enhance the experience.

I used Peco Insulfrog turnouts exclusively for this layout. Insulfrog turnouts have a small bit of plastic at the point of the frog to separate the rails from the two diverging routes, preventing a short circuit. Peco also offers some turnouts in its Electrofrog configuration, which have metal points at the frog, and gaps spaced away from the point to isolate it electrically. You can power the frog with an attached wire using a variety of methods.

You don't have a choice for the curved turnouts, which only come as Insulfog in the code 100 Setrack line, so I used Insulfrog for the others as well. I have not noticed any issues with respect to engine performance

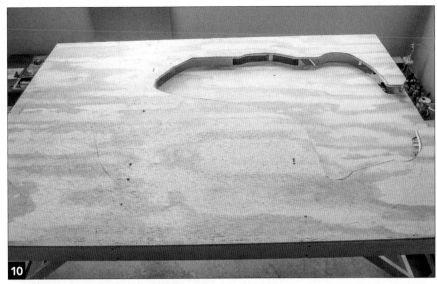

10 I used glue and screws to attach the plywood top to the frame. At this point, the harbor cut-out is temporally positioned.

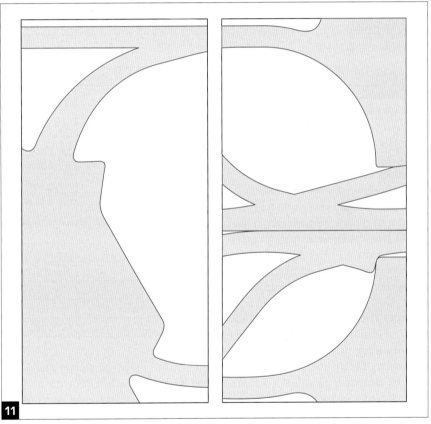

11 This is the approximate cutting pattern for the main sections of roadbed to be cut from the Homasote. The remaining spur sections and road sections can be cut from the leftover pieces of Homasote. This drawing is about 1:12 scale, or 1 inch equals 1 foot.

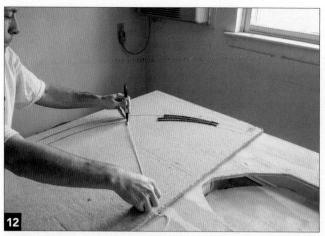

Left: I used an eye-bolt and length of string cut to the curve radius to draw the curved centerlines for the track. Right: I then cut the Homasote with a utility knife.

I cut out sections of the Homasote roadbed to make room for the magnetic uncouplers.

Benchwork materials

Material	Size	Quantity	Purpose
1 x 4 pine	72" long	2	Frame side members
1 x 4 pine	46½" long	4	Frame cross members
1 x 4 pine	1¾" wide pieces about 24" long	4	Harbor supports
2 x 2 pine	40" long	4	legs
2 x 2 pine	3½" long	8	Frame strengthening blocks
1 x 2 pine	48" long	2	Leg lateral bracing
1 x 2 pine	24" long	4	Leg diagonal bracing
Plywood, ½" thick	4 x 6 feet	1	Frame top
Homasote, ½" thick	4 x 4 feet	1	Roadbed
Tempered hardboard, ⅛" thick	2 x 4 feet	1	Harbor base
Swivel casters	1½"	4	Mobility
Wood screws	No. 8 x ¾"	8	For casters
Drywall screws	No. 6 x 1⅝"	1 box	Frame assembly
Wood glue		1 bottle	Frame assembly
¼" bolts and nuts	1½" long	8	Leg attachment
Brads	⅞" x 18	1 pkg.	Homasote

over these turnouts (if anything, the crossovers have shown more issues). Perhaps if you use very short engines you might experience problems; if so, I would avoid using those engines unless you decide to use Digital Command Control (DCC, more on that later) and the decoders have stay-alive capacitors.

Laying the roadbed and track

I've provided a cutting pattern for the roadbed using two 2 x 4-foot pieces of Homasote, **11**. The two pieces are easier to work with than a single 4 x 4-foot piece. I used a utility knife to cut the Homasote. Don't try to cut through the material all at once; use multiple passes of the knife and make sure the blade is sharp. This is quite a workout, but you don't have to worry about dust, as you would if you used the sabre saw.

I drew the track plan onto the Homasote using a black marker with the aid of the scaled track plan as well as positioning track and turnouts on the Homasote. I used an eyebolt attached to a piece of string as a

compass to move the marker along the proper radius and draw the curved sections, **12**. Except for the sections that would be under mountains and hills, I cut the Homasote tight against the track so that later, foam could be butted up against it. You can whittle or carve the edges of the Homosote to resemble rocks or dirt banks; this is especially useful for joining the scenery around the curved tracks near the bridge.

If you want to install uncoupling magnets under the track, cut out rectangular sections in the Homasote

for the magnets, **13**. I placed the magnets on two pieces of cardboard within these cut-out sections to elevate the magnets so they were just touching the underside of the track. Test your rolling stock to ensure the magnetic uncoupling works correctly. You may find uncoupling works better if the magnets are positioned slightly off center, particularly when the magnets are located near a curve. A thin piece of styrene painted brown can be slipped under the track to conceal the magnets.

I glued the Homasote to the plywood subroadbed using wood glue.

This sequence shows the process to cut and insert a straight section of track between turnouts.

I assembled the crossover and turnouts.

I marked the length of the filler piece on the rails.

I cut the rails using a motor tool with a cut-off wheel.

I carefully cut the plastic webs under the rails that connect the ties together, and removed the end ties.

I cleaned up the rail ends using a grinding wheel attachment.

I thinned down extra ties using the grinder attachment.

Once the track was in place, I inserted thinned ties under the rail joiners.

14

This sequence shows the process to install curved sections of track.

I slipped detached ties onto one end of a length of flex track so I could easily remove them later.

I soldered the opposite end of the flex track to a previously laid section of track. In this case it's a turnout.

I curved the flextrack along my guideline and secured it with push pins. I cut the rail ends to join up to track laid previously, and removed ties as necessary.

I removed the pins, added white glue along the guideline, joined the rail ends, replaced the thumbtacks and spiked down the track.

15

A few ¾-inch brads here and there along with some weights (stacks of books) held the Homasote down as the glue dried. The track was then attached to the roadbed using Micro-Engineering medium spikes and white glue.

The first step was to position the turnouts and crossovers, then fill in the gaps. I used a motor tool with a cut-off wheel and grinder attachment to cut and adjust the track for proper fit, **14**. With care, the cut-off wheel can be used to remove end ties so that rail joiners can be inserted onto the rail ends. The grinder attachment is not just useful for fine tuning the track, but also for flattening the excess ties for later insertion underneath the track and rail joiners. Make sure the rail joiners fit tight or you may experience electrical continuity problems later on.

The curved track sections required a little more work. The Peco track does not hold its shape, so it has to be spiked and bent inch by inch along the proper curve. The inner rail will push outward as the track is bent, maintaining contact with the previously laid track, but the outer rail will pull away.

To prevent this, I first soldered the outer rail at one end of the flextrack to a spiked track section. After the track was fully bent, both rails were cut at the far end. Since it is impossible to cut the ties when the track is spiked down, I estimated the length I needed and cut the webs of several of the ties at this location so that each individual tie could be slid off the rails as necessary, **15**.

Test the track as you lay it. You can attach temporary power wires to a short piece of track, attach it to the track you are laying and use a power pack to run an engine and cars back and forth. Check that the train runs smoothly around curves and through turnouts. Also check the magnetic uncoupler operations. I learned that cars may not couple along the curves due to the tight radius. If this happens, a small manual assist will do the trick.

Final wiring on this layout could not be any easier—a grand total of two feeder wires were all that I needed, **16**. I made sure the feeder wires were long enough to reach a power pack placed at either side of the layout. The power pack can either be direct current (DC) or DCC, depending on the type of engine being used.

16

The feeder wires are soldered to the rails.

17

The red arrows indicate possible locations for feeder wires.

Track components		
Component	Part number	Quantity
Curved turnout, right	ST-244 (Insulfrog)	1
Curved turnout, left	ST-245 (Insulfrog)	1
Sharp radius turnout, right	SL-91 Insulfrog	2
Sharp radius turnout, left	SL-92 Insulfrog	3
Short crossover	SL-93 Insulfrog	2
Flextrack, Code 100, 3 ft lengths		8
Flextrack, Code 83, 3 ft lengths		2
Track joiners, metal	Atlas No. 170	1 pkg
Track spikes	Micro Engineering medium, No. 30-104	1 pkg
Kadee permanent under-the-track magnets (optional)	No. 308	4
Wire		1 small roll
Elmers white glue		1 bottle
Rust-Oleum Camouflage Earth Brown spray paint		

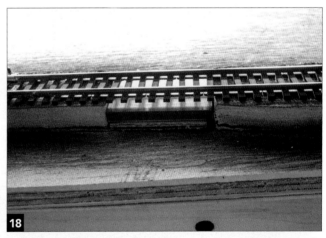

18

A close-up of the painted track over an uncoupling magnet.

I installed the feeders on a section of the layout in view of the operators. You might as well install the feeders on the passing track under the mountain—that way, they won't be seen and you won't have to cover the solder joints. If you do this, make sure to attach one of the feeders to the outside rail of the passing track's outer leg and the other wire to the inside leg's inner rail, **17**. Otherwise, more than two feeder wires will be needed.

Once the track is laid, the wires are connected, and extra ties have been added to fill in gaps, the track may be painted, **18**.

I used a spray can of Rust-Oleum Camouflage Earth Brown to paint the track. I first covered the turnout points and switch rods with masking tape. I then painted the track in short sections, pausing to wipe the paint off the tops of the rails with a cloth rag. After the paint had dried, I touched up the turnouts, then drybrushed the track with light brown chalk to add character and variety to the ties. I also painted some of the ties light brown and gray. Later I'll add dirt, ballast and weeds to finish up the track detailing.

The layout is complete enough to run trains and switch cars while we

dream of bigger things to come. In the next chapter, we'll put on our artist's caps and start realizing the dream by creating a dramatic mountain.

CHAPTER THREE

Beginning scenery: making a mountain

For this layout, the basic construction phases—benchwork, trackwork, and wiring—represent only about 10 percent of the total building time. The remainder of the time is devoted mainly to scenery, structures, and weathering. In most cases, all three activities are performed together: a structure is built and weathered, scenery is created around it in layers, figures and details are added, and final weathering ties it all together. And through the entire process you can be running trains.

A westbound train exits tunnel no. 2 on the way to Northspur. The mountain—tunnel portal included—is a single unit that can be removed for access if necessary.

Let's hear it for scenery

Scenery is probably the most personal aspect to model railroading and one that makes the biggest impact. I imagine those who visited John Allen's famed Gorre & Daphetid RR were awestruck at the sight of floor-to-ceiling mountains with trains hugging cliffsides and precariously crossing bridges and trestles. Close-ups of John's scenery show how meticulous he was in creating his masterpiece, and at one glance of his photographed scenes you knew it was Allen.

Scenery is also enjoyable, satisfying, and connects you to the real world. I find now, having focused on scenery, that I'm more interested and inspired by all sorts of details while walking along outside or driving. These details include the look of the landscape, the shapes and colors of trees, the features on buildings, roads and bridges, all of which are encountered daily.

You don't have to be an "artist" in the usual sense (that is, someone who can draw a person without it looking

2

These are the main tools employed to cut and shape the foam: a small jigsaw and a Stanley Surform rasp. Other useful tools are a hobby knife and a flat file.

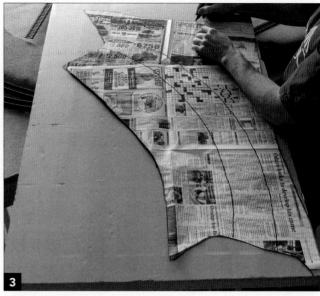

3

I used a newspaper template to trace the first mountain section onto the extruded-foam insulation board for cutting.

like sticks) but it does help to have an artistic eye. Everyone who has imagination and insight can have this; just open up and let it in.

Bob Ross often said while painting, "We have some big decisions to make" and there are none bigger than the type of scenery you wish to create.

I happen to favor Western scenery due to its dramatic possibilities and lively atmosphere. Also, as a model railroader once remarked—upon visiting the Tehachapi Loop in California—"the scenery looks like an inept modeler created it." How sweet is that? You can be inept and still create fine looking Western scenery—no expertise required.

Seriously, I think that remark refers to the coloring, the sparseness of the vegetation and the general barren textures prevalent throughout the landscape. To me, these features add visual interest and, ironically, what might be considered dead is actually full of life.

Instead of wide stretches of nice green grass, you have an interplay of dirt areas, tufts of grass, and weeds. Instead of dense expanses of similar looking green trees, you have a variety of bushes and shrubs growing along hills, ridges, and rocky cliffs, with tall pine trees sprouting up here and there—all of which catch your eye and draw you into the scenes.

Hints on building the scenes

Variation is important to credible scenery, but complete randomness is not. You want some reasonable patterns to the shapes of the hills, rock forms, and vegetation to be convincing. Proper coloring is also extremely important. This is not necessarily easy to do; it helps to study pictures of scenery similar to what you are modeling. Many railroad books are available with plenty of good pictures, or you can simply surf the web using appropriate keywords.

SCENERY TOOLS ➡

- Small hand jigsaw
- Stanley Surform rasp
- Large flat file
- Razor saw
- Tea strainer
- Spray bottle
- Paper cups

Fine art is another useful tool for inspiration. Some time ago, track-planning guru John Armstrong wrote an excellent piece on modeling a diner scene on his Canandaigua Southern O scale layout directly from an Edward Hopper painting. As John pointed out, you'll probably want to avoid the abstractionists and stick with the realists.

There are numerous artists of this school who excelled in outdoor scenes, among them John Constable, Thomas Cole, Albert Bierstadt, and Jacob van Ruisdael. What is gained by studying these artists' works is a good sense of composition, color, textures and lighting that can be used to make your own realistic and interesting scenes. Also, studying such artists is helpful if you want to create effective backdrops.

Using pictures of your own layout while under construction also helps in building effective scenery. That is, formulate a picture you would like to achieve, settle on an appropriate camera angle, stage the scene and keep adding to it until the full picture forms. Such a series of photos allows you to add scenic forms, textures, and details necessary to achieve you vision.

I recommend focusing first on large-order effects—that is, aspects that make the largest impact on the viewer. It also helps to keep a balanced approach and avoid superdetailing some items while leaving other areas barely finished. Generally, a model railroad is only as strong as its weakest features and, unfortunately, the eye is quick to find those features.

Try to avoid "flatness" in your scenery; undulations and hills abound in nature and should be modeled accordingly. The foam sub-base makes this easy to accomplish as you simply

4

The basic mountain has been roughed out. Note that some portions of the mountain extend over the edges of the layout for effect.

5

This is the mold making material, Mold Maker liquid latex rubber from Castin' Craft, that I used to make my rubber mold, right, from the master, left.

cut or carve the foam to achieve the desired look. Roads can also be graduated for best effect. Piles of dirt or other miscellany can also be added to industrial settings to provide texture to the scenes.

For the larger scale rocky areas, I like to create interesting features. Rocks surrounding a tunnel portal, ledges, cuts, and pinnacles are a few examples. You might as well create features with visual impact—it's your world, after all. To that end, you don't need to use pristine "Christmas" trees—besides being easier to make, sparse, non-symmetrical branch structures are found throughout nature and create a more interesting look.

The "Jukes tree," an ancient ponderosa pine with missing branches located north of Chama, New Mexico, on the Denver & Rio Grande Western, was such a tree. Fred Jukes took so many photographs of trains passing by this tree that it took on his name. Other unusual geographic features can add bits of legend to your own layout.

Strategic plan

There are numerous ways to approach building the scenery and structures for the layout. In the coming installments, I will present the strategy I used— working alternatively on scenery and structures, and generally starting with the more challenging parts first. I figure

if I can come through the tougher parts successfully, the remaining parts will not be a problem and I won't have to worry as much. The one exception to this was the water, which needed to wait until the end. Lists of the scenery tools (opposite page) and the general materials I used (page 37) for the entire project are provided.

Forming the mountain

I started the scenery by building the large mountain in the corner of the layout, **1**. This mountain covers the passing track and incorporates two Chooch tunnel portals, one a single cut-stone portal and the other a random stone double portal. I trimmed both portals down about ½-inch (leaving an approximate 3-inch clearance above the track) to keep the mountain more compact.

I built up the mountain using 2-inch thick sections of foam in four separate layers, plus one small piece to form the mesa top. To cut and shape the foam, I used a small jigsaw and a Stanley Surform rasp, **2**. I first made a template of the base using newspaper, then used that template to transfer the pattern onto the foam for the first two layers of the mountain, **3**. The first layer has the middle section entirely cut out to accommodate the track. I carved out a portion of the second layer directly over this to make room for the trains.

I glued the layers together using Liquid Nails For Projects (Aileen's Tacky Glue also works). I continued adding the third and fourth layers, then began cutting and shaping the overall assembly, **4**. I found it convenient to shape the foam on TV dinner stands with newspapers underneath to catch the filings. Compared to the rasp, it's easier to remove material using the jigsaw, but as I found out, it's also easier to remove too much material using the jigsaw! Proceed slowly and you should be fine.

After I established the basic shape and fit the tunnels to the mountain, I began adding rock castings to selected locations. I made the castings using Woodland Scenics lightweight Hydrocal and latex rubber rock molds I had made years ago, **5**. I chose particular rock shapes and sizes to fit the areas I wanted. In the past, I wet-mounted the castings, but this time, I dry-mounted them after they had fully cured.

The advantage of dry mounting is the ease of casting and the ability to take your time positioning the castings. The disadvantage is fitting them to the curvature of the landscape. I used a razor saw to trim the castings for better fit. You can also gently file the castings, or even break them in places for better fits. Be sure to keep all the leftover sections of the plaster castings; these can be used later to represent boulders.

After I removed the plaster rocks from the mold, left, I stained them with colored washes, right.

This sequence shows how I attached the plaster rock castings to the foam mountain.

Top to bottom: First, I cut and filed the foam board mountain surface to accept the casting. I applied Aileen's Tacky Glue to the underside of casting.

With the glue applied, I pushed it into position and held it in place until the glue grabbed.

The castings are in position, along with the tunnel portal. I spray-painted the upper portion of the mountain with a heavy coat of Rust-Oleum Heirloom White to approximate the color of the rock. The lower portions will be painted with craft paints and covered with dirt, gravel, grasses, and shrubs.

I colored the castings using washes of acrylic yellow ochre, raw umber, raw sienna and black, **6**. I also colored some of the individual rock faces within the castings using burnt umber and gray.

I carved notches into the foam to accept the castings, then spray-painted the "rock" portions of the foam with a base coat of Rust-Oleum Heirloom White. This did not cover well, so it took a few thick coats. The paint reacted with the foam to form a hard shell, which is beneficial for approximating rock. Just be careful not to overly deform the areas you notched for the castings.

Once the paint was completely dry, I glued the castings into the notches using Aileen's Tacky Glue, **7**. I then drybrushed the painted foam using Warm Buff, Khaki and Territorial Beige Apple Barrel brand craft paints to blend it in with the castings. I also applied an India ink wash to darken some areas for better blending. Later, I found Rust-Oleum Smoky Beige to be a better base color than the white, as it is a closer match to the colored rocks. A mix of Warm Buff and Dolphin Gray craft paints is also a good color match.

Adding ground cover and vegetation

I removed the mountain from the layout and set it on its side to apply grass and rock talus, **8**. I like to use paper cups or small plastic snack containers to hold various grades of dirt, gravel, grasses and ballast. I place these close at hand to my work area so applications of the ground cover can be easily made.

For the grass, I first applied Woodland Scenics burnt grass fine turf (using my fingers), then a light sprinkling of fine yellow turf on top, and finally some course turf here and there. For the talus I sprinkled some dirt, then poured a layer of Apache Stone from Arizona Rock and Mineral Co. over the dirt. I also used medium buff talus from Woodland Scenics, with some of the talus stained with diluted India ink.

Once I was happy with the lay of the ground cover, I sprayed the area with wet water, consisting of water with some isopropyl alcohol added. I started by spraying upward to let the water droplets descend gently onto the scenery materials, then as the area became wet I aimed the spray more directly.

After this, I soaked the area with a mixture of dilute white glue (about a 60-40 ratio of water to glue). I let the piece dry thoroughly overnight. You may need another treatment to make everything stick, particularly the larger talus.

After the glued dried, I put the mountain back on the layout and began applying small bushes and shrubs. These are made by tearing off small pieces of Woodland Scenics clump foliage, then gluing them into place using white glue. I focused first on areas surrounding the plaster castings to help blend them into the landscape. I also glued some of the bushes onto the castings themselves to further blend the area. I generally decreased the size of the bushes the farther up the slope I went. It takes a long time to plant these bushes, but you can do it while the TV is on in the background, so it isn't too bad.

There are several other methods for blending the rock castings into the terrain. The foam around the casting can be shaped and painted to approximate the rocks. Talus can be spread over the edge of the casting and glued in place to mix in with talus placed below the casting. Larger trees can be planted so as to cross the boundaries of the castings and keep the eye from seeing them.

I added a number of juniper trees to the top of the mountain and some pine trees along the lower edges.

This sequence shows how ground cover was applied to the lower portion of the mountain. Being able to remove the mountain from the layout meant I could lay it on its side to apply the dry ground cover.

Top to bottom: I added Dirt and Apache Stone from Arizona Rock & Mineral Co. to selected areas, then fine ground foam (burnt grass and yellow grass) was applied. Finally, I added some coarse burnt grass turf from Woodland Scenics.

Once I was happy with the look of the ground cover, I saturated the entire area with wet water from a spray bottle, then soaked it with diluted white glue. It's a good idea to label the bottle with a piece of tape to avoid confusion.

More than one application of glue may be necessary. Let the ground cover dry overnight between applications.

8

35

9

I used Woodland Scenics Fine Leaf Foliage for bushes. I've chosen a selection from the package, ready for planting.

I used scissors to prune the Grand Central Gems juniper trees to make smaller and more uniform trees.

10

juniper trees, you can easily prune them using scissors, **10**.

Finishing up

I cut a section of the stone wall to make an abutment for the double tunnel portal, **11**. Later, I used this wall material for the harbor retaining walls as well. You'll note that this wall is O scale; I liked the look of the larger stones, so I went with it. The material is easy to cut using scissors.

I added weathering streaks to the tunnel portals by dipping a wet brush in brown, black and white chalks, then "painting" the portals in vertical lines. I painted the inside of the tunnel with Camouflage Brown spray paint, making it look like a combination of stone and dirt to the casual glance. I'm happy with how the mountain came out. I can lift off the entire piece if need be to access the tracks inside the tunnel or if I someday decide to relocate the layout, **12**.

With an eye-catching natural creation under our belts, next time we'll move to the man-made variety and begin working on structures.

I also mixed in a selection of the fine leaf foliage small trees and shrubs, **9**. This material is delicate, but you can carefully form the trees, poke holes in the foam and glue them into place. This is an expensive material, so I suggest you plant the trees in selected locations. Even so, you should plant several together for best effect. If you want smaller, or more uniform,

11

On the backside of the mountain, I used an O scale stone wall at left and made a pinnacle from foam at the right. Small pieces of clump foliage were used to conceal the seam between tunnel portal and mountain.

Scenery materials

Scenery	Material	Supplier	Quantity
Landforms	Extruded pink foam	DOW Foamular	(1) 2 x 8 ft sheet, 2" thick (1) 2 x 8 ft sheet, 1½" thick
	Foam adhesive	Liquid Nails for Projects or Aileen's Tacky glue	1 tube or bottle
Craft paint	Warm Buff, Dolphin Gray, Khaki, Territorial Beige, Burnt Umber	Apple Barrel	1 bottle each
Spray paint	Heirloom White, Smoky Beige	Rust-Oleum	1 spray can each
Ground cover	Dirt	Natural	As needed
	Crushed leaves	Natural	As needed
	Ground foam, burnt grass, fine	Woodland Scenics	1 small pkg.
	Ground foam, yellow grass, fine	Woodland Scenics	1 small pkg.
	Ground foam, burnt grass, coarse	Woodland Scenics	1 small pkg.
	Talus, buff, medium	Woodland Scenics	1 small pkg.
	Apache stone 1165	Arizona Rock and Mineral Co.	(1) 11-ounce pkg.
	Adhesive	Dilute white glue	1 bottle
Rockwork	Rock molds	As desired	As desired
	Lightweight Hydrocal	Woodland Scenics	½ gallon
	Raw umber + yellow ochre stains	Woodland Scenics	1 bottle each
	India ink + alcohol wash	Homebrew	As needed
Bushes and trees	Clump foliage	Woodland Scenics	1 small pkg.
	Fine leaf foliage	Woodland Scenics	1-2 pkgs.
	Juniper trees	Grand Central Gems	1 bag of 15
	Small pine trees	Grand Central Gems	1 bag of 20
	Apple trees	Grand Central Gems	1 box of 3
	Tall pine trees	Handmade	4
Ballast	Ballast, gray, fine	Woodland Scenics	1 small pkg.
	Ballast, gray, coarse	Woodland Scenics	1 small pkg.
Tunnel portals	Single cut stone	Chooch 8340	1
	Double random stone	Chooch 8370	1
Bridge abutments	Double cut stone	Chooch 8450	1
Stone walls	O scale stone flex wall	Colonial FL7180	1

Finally, the mountain was blended into the layout using ground cover and trees. The mountain is easily removable.

12

CHAPTER FOUR

Scenery and structures: Part 1

Now that we've built a substantial mountain covering the passing track in one corner of the layout, we'll continue adding scenery around the mountain and begin building the structures that will make up Petaluma and Willits.

Supplies are being unloaded on the front dock of Bret's Brewery. In this chapter, we'll learn how to build the structure and detail the surrounding area.

A word about structures

When selecting structure kits for modeling, I'm generally concerned with function, size, appearance and cost. Size is particularly important for small layouts, as you want to balance your scenes while still having a variety of structures.

There are many kit manufacturers. I've selected kits from Campbell Scale Models, American Model Builders (AMB), Fos Scale Models, and Rio Grande Models. These manufacturers offer predominantly wood kits, which I prefer. I find they make for more effective miniatures, are more rustic compared to plastic kits (though plastic represents brick and metal well; the Central Valley bridge, for example, is

excellent). Most of the kits I built were close to plan; others were modified and a few scratchbuilding projects were also undertaken.

Modeling tools and techniques

You don't need a lot of expensive tools or materials to build these models— you can see what I used in the list on page 45. I'm a make-do kind of modeler, and generally use what I have on hand.

For instance, I selected paints for most of the models from my old supply of Polly S paints, but you can find appropriate substitutes using current brands (I'll provide the colors I used). I also didn't have any special work

2 I used a razor saw to add grain to basswood, then I added a weathering wash.

Weathering Chalks

White   Light Brown   Dark Brown   Black

3 I made this selection of weathering chalks by scraping a hobby knife across art store pastel chalks.

4 I used this photo of a local barn as an example for color and texture I wanted to model.

area to build in; I built models on TV dinner stands and stored them under the layout or I built models in the kitchen, standing up at the counter. I also couldn't find my metal ruler and built all the models without one, but even I wouldn't recommend you do that!

I used a few basic weathering methods during construction, including a wash of India ink and alcohol. Many modelers are familiar with this: you simply add a few drops of India ink to a bottle of isopropyl alcohol—the more ink you add, the darker the wash will be. This wash works wonders when weathering wood (there's a tongue twister!), and I used it regularly.

I also used A-West Weather-It (another old product I had in my closet, but now out of production), which works in a similar way. When you stain the wood with these washes, they darken the wood and highlight the grain. After it dries, the wood looks old and gray. From now on when I refer to "weathering wash," I'm referring to the India ink and alcohol stain. Military modelers use a lot of weathering products. You can find them from paint manufacturers such as Acrylicos Vallejo, AK Interactive, and Ammo by Mig Jimenez.

I used basswood and balsa for a variety of models. You can get this

This is the detailing and finishing sequence I used for wood walls.

Top left: I started by distressing the wood boards using hobby knife.

Center left: I darkened the wood with an India-ink/alcohol wash.

Below: I painted individual boards using red acrylics.

Bottom left: I scribed the board joints with the back of a hobby knife for better definition.

Bottom right: Finally, I painted the trim. Now the wall is ready for windows and doors.

5

These are the steps for detailing and finishing stone walls.

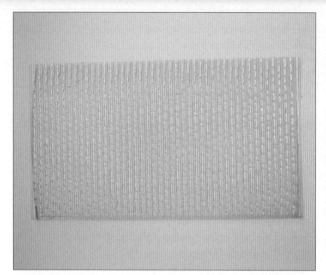

Top left: The raw plastic "stone" sheet is made of clear plastic.

Center left: I spray-painted the sheet gray.

Below: Then I painted individual stones with various earth colors.

Bottom left: I applied DAP spackling to the joints to simulate mortar.

Bottom right: This is the finished wall

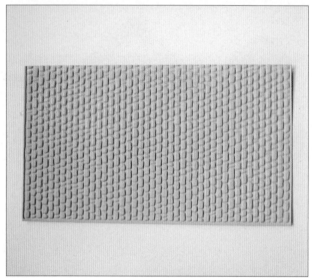

6

wood cheaply at your local hobby store (the total cost of all the wood I used on the layout was about $50). I got plenty of mileage out of 1/16 x 1/8-inch basswood strips; I used these for decks, docks and loading platforms. To texture these pieces, I drew a razor saw across the wood, creating grain, then stained them with the weathering wash, **2**.

Another staple of weathering models is pastel chalk. I used inexpensive pastel chalks you can find at art stores. I used four main colors: white, light brown, dark brown and black. When I wanted to use them, I scraped the chalk with a hobby knife blade, forming a small pile on a piece of paper, **3**. I then brushed the chalks on the model, either dry or with a brush dipped in water or alcohol. The latter method is good for getting the chalks to stick to particular areas versus an overall dusty look.

One last useful technique is drybrushing. Most modelers are familiar with this. Dip a brush in paint and drag the brush over paper until most of the paint is gone. Then brush the model to add highlights or subtle weathering patterns. This technique is particularly good for locomotives and rolling stock.

Building the structures

Now I'll discuss how I built the structures that make up Petaluma and Willits, starting with Bret's Brewery. This kit, produced by Campbell Scale Models, yields a model with loads of character. It caught my eye 20 years ago and I bought it without any particular plan for it. Now I think it makes a fine addition to Petaluma on this layout.

I think one of the most important features of a model is its color scheme. Before beginning construction, I consider what colors to use, not only with respect to the model itself but also with respect to other models on the layout. You want some distinction to each model but not a wild variation among models, otherwise the eye will revolt and see them all as one.

Bret's Brewery

I often take pictures of prototype buildings and scenery to help with the

The detailing and finishing sequence for roof shingles.

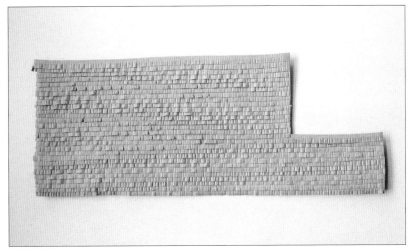

First, I applied the Campbell shingles to the cardstock roof material supplied in the kit.

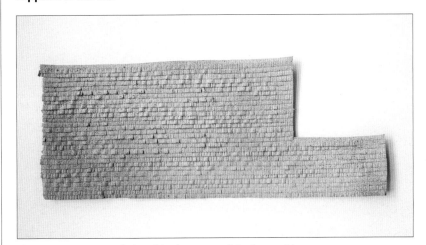

Then I spray-painted the shingles gray with shots of brown.

Finally, I weathered the roof using a brush and light brown chalk.

7

This sequence shows how to add windows and shades.

First, I installed the windows in an assembled wall section.

I glued clear styrene and paper shades to backside.

The finished windows, glass, and shades complete the wall assembly.

8

9

At first I wasn't satisfied with the roof on the finished model of Willits Station. While I thought about replacing it, its appearance grew on me.

color selections. In the case of Bret's Brewery, I had some pictures of red barns that I liked and patterned the model accordingly, **4**.

Bret's Brewery will take some time to build as it contains many components. The instructions and plans are accurate and detailed; I suggest reading through them thoroughly and getting comfortable with the design before you start to build.

You may decide to make some modifications. I did not follow all the steps in the order given in the instructions, as I wanted to prepare the components separately before assembling them. This makes it easier to work on and weather the parts, but it also means you will have to wait a while to see the structure come together.

Let's see how I built and weathered the various components.

Foundation and docks: For the look of worn and weathered wood, I applied the weathering wash. It's best to apply the wash before gluing the parts together. Most glues will seal the wood and prevent stain from coloring it. I also used "wet chalk" applications of brown and black to selective boards to further distinguish them.

Wood walls: I first distressed the wood wall pieces using a hobby knife in select locations, then applied the weathering wash, **5**. After this had dried, I applied red acrylic paints (Boxcar Red and Rock Island Maroon) with a brush in various consistencies. I generally applied thicker paint nearer the tops of the walls and thinner paint nearer the bottoms, letting some of the gray wood show through.

I figure that paint would weather more near the bottom of a building

where the elements and rain have greater impact. Once the paint had dried, I used a hobby knife to cut along the grooves between wood boards, giving more definition to them. Lastly, I painted the trim.

Stone walls: This kit contains plastic impressed "stone" sheets. I first painted these sheets with gray Rust-Oleum primer, then used a brush to paint individual stones a variety of earthen colors: beige, earth and aged concrete, **6**. To create mortar, I used DAP lightweight spackling compound.

I added this into the spaces between the stones with my fingers, then wiped it clear of the stone faces. The spackling also helped to conceal the seams when the wall segments are joined together.

Shingled roofs: First, I applied the Campbell shingles per the instructions, **7**. Next, I spray-painted the roof with gray primer and several shots

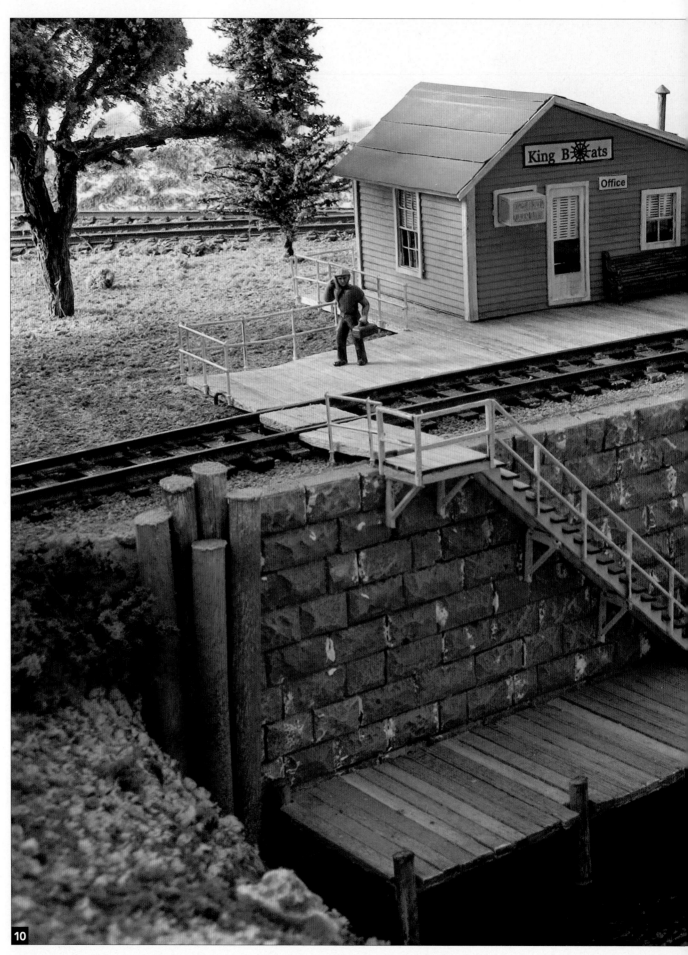

King's boathouse is situated on the Petaluma harbor. I repurposed an AMB yard office for nautical duty and added an access to the dock.

I used newspaper trimmed to fit between track roadbed to create templates for the foam terrain.

of Rust-Oleum Camouflage Earth Brown to create some variations. For further variations and highlights, I drybrushed light brown chalk into the shingles. Once the roofing was attached to the building, I applied more chalks to simulate dirt and soot streaks from the chimney and also white streaks here and there. White bird droppings and streaks can be seen all around in nature.

Aluminum roofs: After cutting the corrugated aluminum to size using a hobby knife, I spray-painted it with clear flat spray to give something for the paint to stick to. I then used Oxidized Aluminum paint (can be approximated with a mixture of silver and black) with drybrushed streaks of red and brown to color the roof. I used Aileen's Tacky Glue to affix the panels to the cardboard roof sections.

Trim: I spray-painted the windows and plastic trim material Rust-Oleum Heirloom White, then applied an India ink wash to further age these pieces.

I brushed the building's wood trim with Aged White and Reefer White to approximate the window colors.

Windows: I placed clear styrene sprayed with a flat finish behind the windows to simulate dirty glass, **8**. I glued this material over the entire window area, which is simpler than trying to glue the styrene into the window frames. This is only possible if you do not wish to detail the interior of the building and will not have clear view of the inside. I also glued file folder material darkened with the weathering wash behind the windows to simulate window shades.

The lead photo, **1**, shows the finished model from the front, highlighting the various component materials. I added details to the scene, including a small transfer platform, boxes, barrels, pallets, trucks, and figures.

Willits Station

I used the AMB Northern Pacific Class C Depot for the Willits station.

This kit features laser-cut, notched wood walls and peel and stick trim, windows, and shingles. Laser-cut kits such as this are about as easy to build as a plastic kit, especially with peel-and-stick windows and trim.

However, working with the peel-and-stick parts can sometimes be frustrating as they are delicate and you need to be careful when placing them to get the best appearance. I suggest using a hobby knife to start pulling the backing off, being careful not to pull the sticky material completely off. The small windowsills had lost their stickiness, so I used small pieces of stripwood as a substitute.

I also suggest checking the peel-and-stick material before painting to make sure you are not painting the backing. I checked the shingle strips, but not the flashing, and guess which ones I had to repaint? Luckily there was only a small amount of flashing.

I wanted to paint the station with a color scheme similar to the Ridgeway station on the Rio Grande Southern: cream walls, brown trim, and dark red shingles, **9**. The Polly Scale colors I used were Aged White, Earth and PRR Tuscan. When I first put the roof on, I was not too pleased with the look, but after a few days it grew on me and now I like it. Lesson learned: if you are unhappy with some part of a model that is not easy to change, live with it a day or two and your happiness level may increase. If you are still unhappy, you can then bite the bullet and make the change.

One aspect of the roof that I am still unhappy about is my lack of discipline in placing the shingles. I am used to Campbell shingles, which look good as long as you place them in reasonably straight rows, but the AMB shingles are slightly larger and more regular and look best if you offset them between rows such that every other row is aligned. It is not something you see at lower viewing angles, but is apparent looking straight down. I'll live with it for now.

The AMB kits contain brown peel-and-stick window material. If you like the color, you can use the material as is, which saves effort painting it. For two of the kits—this one and the Tiburon

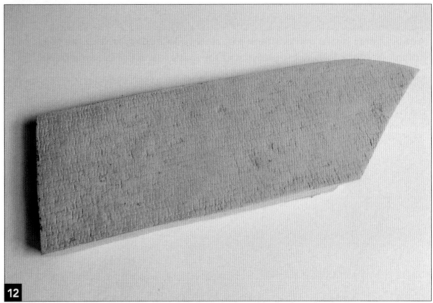

12 I used Homasote cut to form road sections. The lip fits up to the track.

tower—I used a near-match brown acrylic paint to lightly brush over the peel-and-stick material, providing some variation and creating a more weathered appearance. If you want to change the color, you will need to paint the peel-and-stick material with several heavier coats of your desired color.

I painted this model to represent a fairly well-maintained station. I lightly weathered the model by adding light brown chalk streaks along the roof and some black chalk along the walls. I needed to be careful; if you touch a brush to black chalk and then touch it to the model you will get a thicker splotch of black than you probably want, and it is difficult to spread it evenly.

A better technique is to load the brush, then touch it a few times to a scrap piece of paper to remove some chalk, then lightly brush it on the model. This is similar to drybrushing; perhaps we can call it dry-chalk brushing?

I made station signs using Microsoft Word, printed them out on white paper, cut them using scissors and glued them to the building using a thin coat of white glue. I also attached the Railway Express Agency signs supplied with the kit using thin white glue.

This kit does not include a loading platform; I made one by cutting a piece of 1/32-inch thick basswood into

13 I cut insulation board and positioned it, along with a road, around the track and structures. Bret's Brewery is placed and the station is under construction.

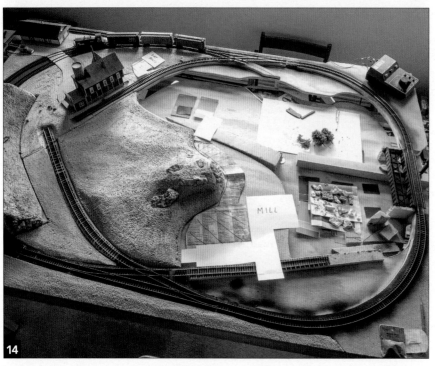

14 I added more foam terrain around Northspur, and inserted some rock castings into the central hill. Note the paper footprint for the sawmill: I used this to help position the landscape and roads.

in front. I placed a bench and a few figures on the platform to add some life to the scene.

Boathouse

I wanted a "nautical" structure to help set the tone in Petaluma. I built AMB's yard office as a boathouse, with a walkway leading across the brewery spur and down a flight of stairs to a dock in the harbor below, **10**.

I mixed a light blue color for the boathouse using C&O Enchantment Blue and Reefer White. I used Reefer White for the trim and Grimy Black for the roofing. I made a sign in Word and glued it to the front of the building.

I constructed the deck and walkway from ⅛-inch basswood strips glued together along their edges. I sanded the foam layout surface to allow the walkway to sit level. I added Tichy pipe railings (no. 8013) around the deck, painted white. I placed AMB stairs (no. 332) against a cut stone wall leading down to the dock, which I built from ⅛-inch basswood strips and ⅛-inch dowels. I don't know the exact brand of rock wall (again, it was in my scrap box) but you should do fine using a Chooch wall or a similar product.

Shaping the landscape

After finishing Bret's Brewery, I began adding landscaping around the structure by inserting sections of extruded foam between the track roadbed.

When placing the foam terrain before all the relevant models are built, it helps to use paper cutouts as stand-ins for the models and roads. Simply refer to the kits and determine the footprint dimensions, then cut out the corresponding paper shapes. These can be placed on the layout to help you figure out how you want the landscape to look in the context of the structures. I used newspaper to create the templates for the foam inserts, **11**.

Generally, I cut a 12-inch-wide section of 1½-inch-thick foam in half to make two ¾-inch-thick pieces. I then used the templates to trace the pattern onto the foam with a black Sharpie and finally cut out the pieces.

approximately ⅛-inch thick planks and gluing these planks to a frame made from ⅛-inch basswood (you'd be better off using stock ⅛-inch basswood strips instead of cutting them). The station was then placed on top of the frame with the platform

It may take several pieces to make up the entire area. The top surface is easily shaved to the appropriate height, aligning with the roadbed under the track and rising or falling naturally in places away from the track.

The gaps between foam pieces or between the foam and roadbed may be patched with lightweight spackle. I used Aileen's Tacky Glue to fill in the small seams; for larger gaps I first filled them with thin pieces of foam, then applied the spackle over the top. You can also use small sections of foliage clusters to fill in the gaps.

Roads

Homasote makes for effective roads. The material may be cut to the desired shape using a utility knife, then sanded with fine sandpaper to remove the top scale, leaving a smoother gray top surface. The dings and imperfections in the Homasote should be left in as such features are often seen in most roads. The roads can be left as is to simulate concrete (a small hacksaw can be used to add expansion joints), or sprinkled with dirt to simulate dirt roads. I applied black chalk to simulate faded asphalt.

For grade crossings, the ends of the Homasote road pieces can be notched to sit over the outer ties, leaving a small gap between the ends of the roads and the rails, **12**. A small section of Homasote can be cut and trimmed to fit between the rails. I like this method because it allows for dry fitting of the roads with no mess compared to the "wet" plaster and putty methods. When you are happy with the fit, you can glue the road in place, or leave it unglued as I did, **13**.

Color and texture

I painted the foam terrain with inexpensive craft paints from Apple Barrel. My final recipe for dirt and rock was an equal mixture of Warm Buff and Dolphin Gray. I added a little water and applied this over the foam using a paintbrush. I also added Khaki and applied this in areas to simulate browner earth and burnt grass areas. This treatment goes a long way in creating a natural Western landscape.

15

This sequence shows how to install uncoupling magnets and detail track.

The Kadee uncoupling magnet is set on cardboard spacers below track.

A thin piece of styrene painted brown is slipped under the rails to cover the magnet. Then I added the foam terrain.

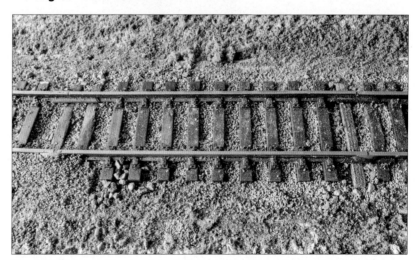

Here's the scene after I painted the foam terrain and added dirt, ballast and ground foam.

These are the steps I followed to apply landscape scenery.

I painted the foam with a mix of brown and gray paints and filled some of the gaps in the foam with lightweight spackle. In other places, I filled gaps between the foam and track using small clumps of foliage clusters.

This is what the area looked like after adding ground cover and ballast.

16

I soaked the area with diluted white glue.

This is the area after the glue dried. There's no sign of the glue, yet the materials are firmly attached.

This shows the same area after adding trees, foliage, the road, and structures.

You could even dab areas with green paint to create grassy regions. In this way, an effective landscape can be created using nothing but paint and roughened foam.

Once the paint is dry, I added dirt, ground foam, and ballast, **15-16**. I generally sprinkle fine ground foam (burnt grass, then some yellow grass) over the general area (leaving bare spots as well), then pat down coarse burnt grass ground foam in particular areas to simulate taller grass and weeds.

For ballast, I used a mixture of backyard fine dirt and Woodland Scenics fine gray ballast, with some sprinkles of coarse gray ballast along the sides of the track. I also used dirt alone for the logging and sawmill spurs. I passed the dirt through a tea strainer to remove the larger particles. I again used my wet water solution, followed by diluted white glue to fix everything into place, applying the glue solution liberally.

I sanded the painted foam with a fine sanding block to create small dirt roads and bare dirt areas. Small pieces of plaster rocks were inserted into the foam by cutting out small sections (or filing the castings) and

pushing the castings into place. By adding course turf, dirt, and gravel around these rocks, I blended them into the landscape. Talus can be spread in some areas as well. The idea is to get variations in the shape of slopes, and in textures and colors.

You can repeat this process as many times as you need to get the look you're after. You can also add larger foliage clusters to simulate bushes, as well as fine leaf foliage and trees. Trees are best inserted by simply pushing their wire trunks into the foam; in this way, you can change their locations in the future if you wish.

After the glue dried, I had to clean the track to get back to operation. I scraped the tops of the rails with a fingernail to remove residual glue and applied Robart Manufacturing's Rail-zip track cleaner to the rails. It took a while to get the locomotive to run smoothly, particularly over the crossover tracks.

We've made a good start on the scenery and structures. We'll continue next time pushing out to Fort Bragg.

CHAPTER FIVE

Scenery and structures: Part 2

The corners on a rectangular layout featuring a loop are substantial areas, but difficult to make use of. In the last two installments, I showed how to cover one corner with a large mountain and insert a station into another. Now I'll describe how to fill the remaining two corners with rocky hills, simulating a canyon with a bridge between them.

This is the back side of the sawmill-lumber yard complex at Fort Bragg. In this chapter, I'll build the sawmill and detail the area around Fort Bragg, including the Noyo Canyon hills seen in the background.

The method for building the hills is the same as for the large mountain, just at a smaller scale, **1**. I built up the hills using foam in layers, then shaped the overall form with the Surform tool. The layers were glued together, then selected plaster castings, ground cover and vegetation were added. For interest, I carved a lookout trail into one of the hills and a rock cut into the other one.

Between the hills is the opening for the harbor. I installed a Central Valley through plate girder bridge to carry the tracks across the water. The Central

Valley bridge kit went together easily. I was able to push two code 100 rails through enough of the plastic "spikes" on the deck to hold the rails in place (the spikes are sized for code 83 rail).

I painted the bridge with Rust-Oleum Camouflage Black and the deck Camouflage Earth Brown. To weather the bridge, I used chalks, **2**. First, I used a brush (medium stiffness) to apply light brown chalk to the bridge side panels and worked the powders in with the brush and my fingers. I also did this for the ties on the deck.

This is the hill construction sequence.

Top left: I cut the foam roughly to shape and positioned it on the layout as I worked out the contours.

Center left: Further shaving to the foam finalizes the hill shape.

Below: I added plaster castings to recesses in the hillside.

Bottom left: I gave the foam a heavy coat of Smoky Beige paint.

Bottom right: I added ground cover and vegetation to blend the rock castings into the hillside. The opposite hillside is under construction with a Central Valley bridge in the center.

1

This is the bridge weathering sequence.

I brushed light brown chalk onto the black-painted sides of bridge to create a fade.

I dipped a wet brush in dark brown chalk and brushed along the rivet strips to simulate rust.

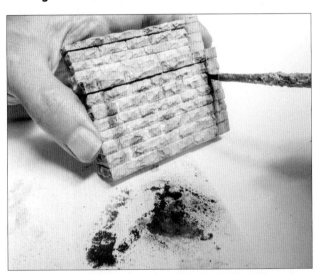

Wet chalks brushed onto the abutments simulates rust and other deposits. Note the small section of carved balsa on the right side to extend the abutment for better bridge positioning.

This is the finished weathering of the bridge and abutment.

2

Next, I dipped the brush in water, touched it to dark brown chalk and applied this to the vertical line of rivets on the panel connectors and the lower edge of the bridge side panels. When the water dries, the chalk is left where you applied it.

For the abutments, I cut a Chooch double abutment to the proper height and then cut it in half vertically. The two pieces served to support the bridge

with the cut sections facing away from the harbor. The two halves were a little narrow, so I glued thin sections of carved balsa to the cut abutment edges to provide a bit more width.

I painted some of the stones a variety of gray and concrete colors, then used the wet chalk technique to add rust streaks and white streaks over multiple stones. The bridge is easily removed from the layout by sliding the

end rail connectors under the adjoining track sections and lifting the bridge off the abutments.

Fort Bragg development

Continuing on, I developed terrain for the Fort Bragg area. I made a paper footprint of the sawmill and set it in place on the layout to help define the location of the spur track, road and landscape, **3**. To form the road,

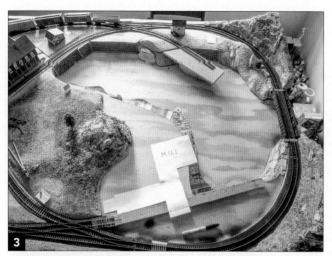

This top view of the layout shows my progress at six months into the project. I'm halfway through!

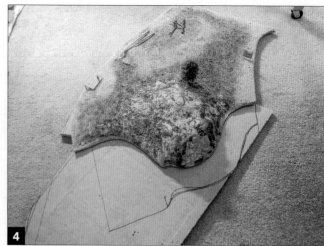

Foam scenery was used to trace out the road on scrap piece of Homasote.

The road is in place and foam pieces have been inserted to help define Fort Bragg. Next to come is the large sawmill-lumber yard complex.

I removed the adjoining foam landform and used it to trace out the left side of the road, **4**. The location of the sawmill primarily defined the end, and the right side follows a logical line for the road.

After positioning the road, I filled in the remaining areas with foam, **5**. Later, when I was fully happy with the landscape, I glued the foam down using Tacky Glue. I did not glue the roads

down in case I want to remove them.

Sawmill and lumber yard

To build the sawmill-lumber yard, I started with Campbell's Saez Sash

Sawmill construction sequence is as follows:

I built a simple foundation for the sawmill using 1/8-inch square basswood. The sawmill adjoins the Campbell kit's overflow shed.

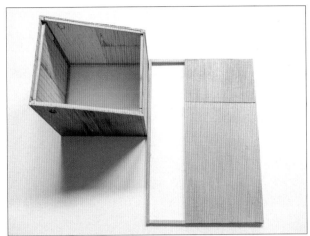

I added scribed siding for the floor of the shed where it would be visible through the door. I later added cardboard to fill the remaining section.

This is the scribed siding after applying Weather-It and streaks of black and brown chalks. The bottom edges were distressed with a hobby knife prior to weathering.

The walls were added to the floor.

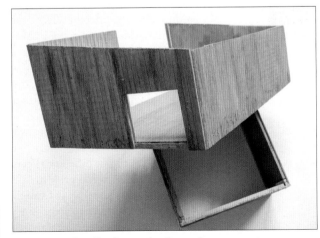

This view of walls shows the front door cut out.

This view of backside shows the door and upper wood rail applied.

Sawmill roof construction sequence is as follows:

I applied strips of black tissue paper to represent tarpaper roofing on the sawmill.

This is the roof after painting and brushing with light brown chalks.

and Door kit, reversing the positions of the lumber shed and maintenance shed with respect to the overflow shed (I used the overflow shed as a steam power station).

I left most of the back wall off the lumber shed to allow for loading from both sides. I figured that fresh-sawn lumber could be placed in the lumber shed from the back, and this lumber could later be loaded into boxcars from the front.

I used Weather-It and my India ink weathering wash to color the wood, and did not paint over this to create a more raw appearance. For further variation, I applied some wet brown and orange chalk to some of the boards.

I built the sawmill using basic wood components, **6**. I first formed the foundation from ⅛-inch square basswood, then added scribed siding (¹⁄₁₆-inch spacing x ¹⁄₃₂-inch thick) and cardboard sections for the floor. I used scribed siding (⅛-inch spacing x ⅛-inch thick) for the walls.

I distressed some of the siding boards using a hobby knife, particularly near the bottom edges. When Weather-It and weathering washes were applied, these distressed sections became more prominent. I likewise distressed the wall where the sliding rear door would naturally scratch indentations in the wood. I used the sliding door from the Campbell kit, moving it from the overflow shed to the sawmill building.

The Weather-It and India ink produce slightly different effects; the India ink yields a "grayer" look. Also, not all wood is uniform in density and will take the stains differently, yielding some color variations. Generally, this is a good thing, particularly for a sawmill where a variety of wood was used for construction and not all sections were built at one time.

I've noticed I got different effects if I distressed the wood prior to staining vs. after staining. If I wanted the distressed features to stand out, I stained after distressing; for a more subtle appearance, or to depict recently scratched surfaces, I distressed the wood after staining.

I found another effective way of weathering wood is to drybrush Pavement craft paint onto the wood pieces after they had been lightly stained with India ink.

I attached a smokestack (⅛-inch diameter aluminum tube painted black) to the shed adjoining the sawmill. This adds visual interest and indicates the location where power is generated for the saws.

I connected the chip conveyer piping from the sawmill to the elevated hopper, allowing wood chips generated in the mill to be transported to the hopper for later unloading into hopper cars. I added small wood support structures for the smokestack and chip conveyer piping. These and other roof details are nice to add whenever possible since the roof is highly visible.

I used black tissue paper on the sawmill roof, **7.** I cut the tissue paper into strips about ½-inch wide, then laid the strips in rows on a piece of cardboard, slightly overlapping each row, then attached them with white glue. After the glue dried, I sprayed on Rust-Oleum Camouflage Earth Brown and over-brushed the paint with light brown chalk for a dusty look.

I added small pieces of non-weathered roof paper strips here and there to represent newly repaired sections, and added a number of roof vents. I made the vents from ⅛-inch dowel; some of them I topped with a wrapping of ⅛-inch strips of masking tape and others with small ovals of paper curved over the tops. I painted the vents black and brushed on some rust colored chalk to weather them.

I created the logs for the mill using ⅜-inch or ½-inch square balsa, **8.** I cut the wood to the appropriate length, then whittled the basic log shape using a utility knife.

After some light sanding, I scored the wood using a razor saw to model bark texture. Then I applied a wash of acrylic burnt umber along with some Weather-It stain to color the logs. After the paint was dry, the log ends were cut to give the appearance of saw cuts. To model the logs floating in the

How to shape, texture and color balsa wood to simulate logs or tree trunks.

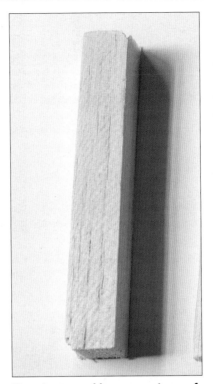
First, I cut roughly square pieces of balsa to length.

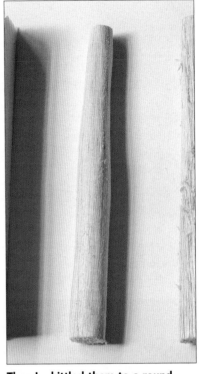
Then I whittled them to a round shape with a utility knife.

I scored them with a razor saw blade.

And finally, I stained them with a wash of acrylic burnt umber and Weather-It.

8

This sequence highlights construction of the log unloading station.

A view from the harbor shows the sawmill spur and steep bank down to the log pond

I added the logs one at a time. The logs to the right will be set so the top log is positioned just below the height of the flatcar delivering the load.

The final shot of log dump shows how unloaded flatcars just fit under the poke, at left.

9

All the primary logs are in place. Another log will be placed at an angle against the taller logs at left to form the "poke" across the tracks.

harbor, I cut them in half lengthwise and placed them on top of the modeled water.

This general approach is also useful for creating full-size tree trunks and stumps around the layout.

I built a log unloading station using a wall of logs and a poke to force the logs over the wall into the harbor, **9**. This arrangement is similar to that employed by the Santa Cruz lumber Company in California.

I fashioned a jack-slip to pull the logs from the harbor into the sawmill, which extends over the harbor banks on wood pilings. I made the jack-slip from basswood. It is composed of a scaffold, a long chute and an adjoining ladder with handrail, **10**.

I also fashioned some simplified saw tables to fit inside the sawmill near the open door. I did not over-detail the interior, just enough to provide a sense of equipment when looking through

10

I made the jack-slip using basswood and balsa.

For the spurs, I removed some of the ties from a section of code 83 track, then trimmed and painted the ties (bottom). An unmodified section of code 83 track is in the upper left and a section of code 100 track is shown in the upper right.

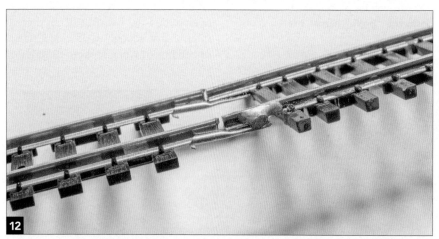

To join code 83 track, right, to code 100 track, install a rail joiner on the code 100 track, flatten it with pliers, then solder the code 83 track to the flattened rail joiner.

This close-up view of joint on layout shows how it looks after scenery is applied.

The McGiffert log loader straddles the track with its wheels retracted, ready to accept a string of flat cars for loading.

15

The landscape around the harbor was formed the same way as the rest of the layout. Hooper's Oysters will be placed in the center by the road.

the door from normal viewing angles. I placed a small awning over the door, which further obscures the view.

I used code 83 track for the logging spurs. I removed about a quarter of the ties, then spread out the remainder to create a sparser look, **11**. Most railroad sidings have fewer ties per yard than mainline tracks. I also clipped the ends from some of the ties for a less uniform look. I painted some of the ties slightly different colors than the standard brown.

To join the code 83 track with the code 100 track, I flattened the rail joiners coming off the code 100 track, laid the code 83 rails on top of

the flattened sections, then soldered the rails to the joiners, **12**. It may look messy (and perhaps I am not the neatest solderer) but after dirt and ballast is applied, you can hardly see the joint unless you really look for it, **13**.

McGiffert Loader
This is largely a cast metal kit, which requires cyanoacrylate adhesive (CA) for assembly, **14**. You might want to consider an accelerator to cure the glue, as it took a long time for the glue to set on its own. If you want to build the loader so flat cars can run under it (a prototypical loading practice), attach the support structure higher up on the

legs. I am using low-profile flat cars and they just barely clear the supports.

I painted the lower metal parts using Rust-Oleum Camouflage Brown spray paint. I used oxidized aluminum paint for the winch assembly. I fashioned a simple roof covering with as much open side space as possible to allow a view of the winches and steam tank. A general drybrushing of brown and black completed the weathering.

Hooper's Oysters
I wanted to place an interesting structure along the harbor bank near the center of the layout and chose Hooper's Oysters from Fos Scale,

These are the steps I followed while working with corrugated roofing strips for Hooper's Oysters.

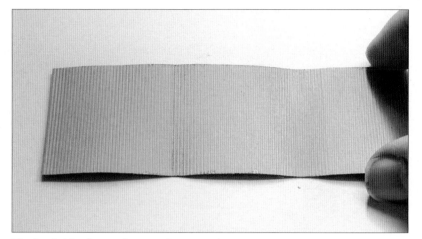

The backside shows the wood corrugation.

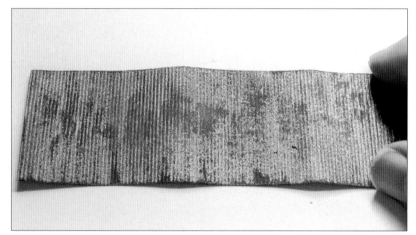

I painted the strips with oxidized aluminum paint, then streaked the pieces with brown.

15-17. This structure has character, plenty of detail, and allows modeling down to the water with stilt supports and a fishing barge.

I used heavy drybrush applications of reefer white over the walls to simulate worn, weather-beaten paint. The supplied corrugated roofing material is different than I'm used to; most kits offer metal corrugated panels. But this kit had wood corrugated strips. The wood strips are easier to paint and glue down compared to the metal panels, **16**.

For a convincing worn metal look, I first primed the wood strips using gray Rust-Oleum spray paint, then brushed on Polly S oxidized aluminum, and followed this with a drybrushing of

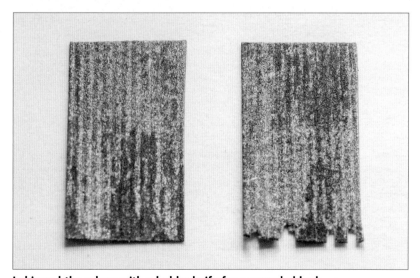

I chipped the edges with a hobby knife for a corroded look.

16

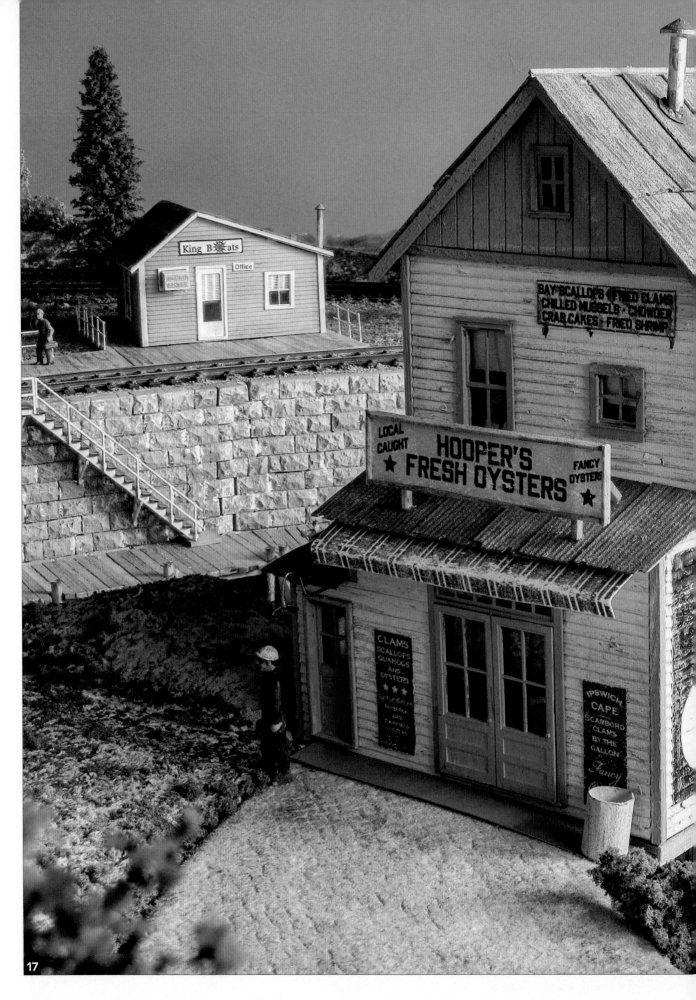

King B[oa]ts

Office

BAY SCALLOPS · FRIED CLAMS
CHILLED MUSSELS · CHOWDER
CRAB CAKES · FRIED SHRIMP

LOCAL
CAUGHT

HOOPER'S
★ FRESH OYSTERS

FANCY
OYSTERS

★

CLAMS
SCALLOPS
QUAHOGS
AND
OYSTERS

★ ★ ★

IPSWICH
CAPE
SCARBORO
CLAMS
BY THE
GALLON

Fancy

17

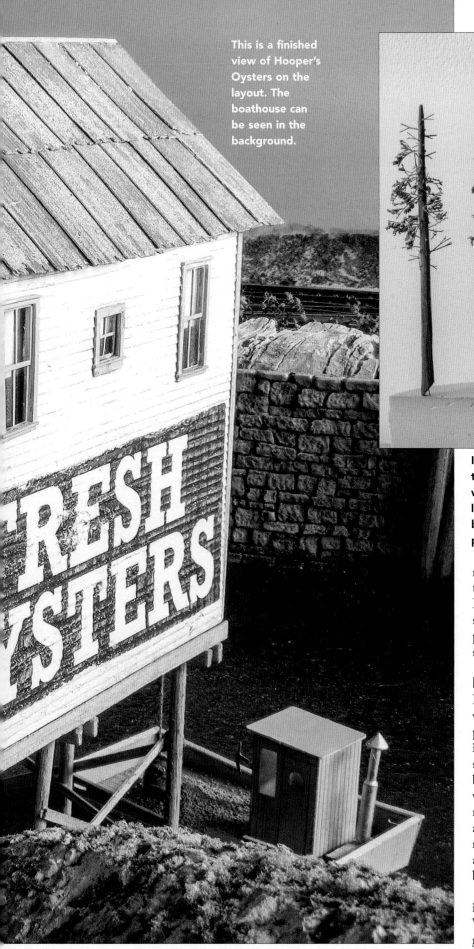

This is a finished view of Hooper's Oysters on the layout. The boathouse can be seen in the background.

I handmade my pine trees using balsa trunks and caspia branches. There were a few varieties, including from left: a "dying" tree, a tree made using bunch caspia, and a tree made using pressed caspia.

roof brown, streaking and blotching the paint to create a rusty appearance. I also cut the bottom edges of the strips to simulate metal erosion. Silver paint with some black mixed in can be substituted for the oxidized aluminum.

Lodgepole pines

No Western layout is complete without at least a few tall lodgepole or ponderosa pines. I made these trees by inserting dried caspia branches into a stained balsa trunk, then painted the branches brown and sprinkled them with green ground foam, **18**. You don't need that many branches to make an effective tree. I will note that my recent batch of caspia was pressed flat and does not look quite as good as the bunch variety.

In the next chapter, I'll move out into the harbor and model some water. We're getting near the end. Is that a good thing or a bad thing?

CHAPTER SIX

Scenery and structures: Part 3

There has been a lot of progress so far and I've completed most of the ground work. Now, I'll focus on modeling the water areas, starting with the Tiburon pier.

The pier in Tiburon is busy with unloading activity. In this chapter, we'll learn how to model both the pier and the harbor using inexpensive, simple methods.

I built the pier from ³⁄₁₆-inch diameter wood dowels (for pilings), ³⁄₁₆-inch square basswood (for support beams) and ⅛-inch x ¹⁄₁₆-inch basswood strips (for planking), **1**. I built it in place, measuring the necessary dimensions as I went, **2**.

First, I cut the crossbeams and support pilings to size, then stained all the pieces with Weather-It and/or the weathering wash. I also drybrushed the pilings with Pavement and Antique White craft paints for a more weather-worn appearance. After the pieces were dry, I glued five pilings to each crossbeam to create the pier footing assemblies.

I drew a razor saw across the

1

The wood components for the pier include a package of dowels from Walmart and basswood from the hobby shop.

This is the construction sequence for building the pier:

I cut and weathered nine support beams and 45 pilings.

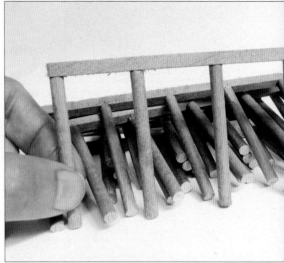

I glued five pilings to each support beam to complete the footing assemblies.

All nine footing assemblies and deck support beams have been added, along with track and track supports.

2

I began on-site construction of the pier using two side beams and the first and last footing assemblies. The finished interlocking tower can be seen in the background, near a stone retaining wall.

The deck is completed. Bumper and side pilings are being positioned.

planking strips to add grain before staining them; this adds a lot of character to the deck. I applied the deck boards one by one on top of the frame rather than use scribed siding. It's a slower process, but you can create a more realistic appearance by leaving gaps between some of the boards, damaging boards and even using different wood to simulate repairs.

I set the planking between the rails in the direction of the rails rather than across the rails (in the direction of the main deck). It is much easier to lay the planks between the rails this way, and it's the way the prototype would do it. I used ³⁄₃₂-inch basswood strips under the track to allow the planking to sit level across the support beams and just under the rail height. You may have to adjust the size of the strips if you use different track than I did.

After completing the main structure, I added some short bumper pilings in front and some taller edge pilings along the more exposed side of the pier to allow boats to dock. I added a small shed from the Campbell Quincy module sheds kit to the end of the wharf to represent a storage area. I also added a modified version of the Campbell Quincy traveling crane, providing a visible means of unloading and transferring freight and equipment from the railroad cars.

I scattered a number of crates, wood pieces, barrels and chains to the pier deck and added some figures to complete the scene. I made the crates by cutting ½-inch square balsa into ½-inch sections, then applying the weathering wash. The end grain takes a darker stain than the sides and looks like the tops and bottoms of wood crates.

You'll notice in the pictures how the pier fits up against a rocky bank. On either side of the pier and bank, I placed rock retaining walls fronted with wood pilings, **3**. The retaining walls are made of flexible resin and may be cut to size using scissors. I brushed over the dark gray stones with a wash of Warm Buff craft paint to add texture and highlights to the stones. I used a hobby knife blade to cut and chip at the stones here and there for variety.

This close-up of the rock retaining wall shows the wood pilings. The ropes are made from heavy thread.

All the scenery and structures adjoining the water have been completed. Now all that's needed is the water.

WATER MATERIALS ➡

- Hardboard, 2 x 4 feet
- Apple Barrel Multi-Surface paints:
  - Black
  - Primary Blue
  - Mountain Forest Green
- Gloss Mod Podge
- Medium paint brushes (flat and round)

I used ³⁄₁₆-inch diameter wooden dowels for support pilings and tie-off pilings. These can be purchased cheaply at a department store craft department. I cut the tops of the dowels at varying angles, split some of the tops, and hit them with a hammer or a large wood file to simulate natural weathering. I stained the dowels with the weathering wash, then drybrushed them with Pavement and Antique White craft paint. I wrapped string around some of the dowels to represent ropes.

I built the AMB Yard Office kit and placed it near the pier to represent an interlocking tower. I painted the walls Reefer White and the roof and trim Roof Brown. I weathered the walls with a light application of black chalk and the roof with light brown chalk.

Modeling the water

Now I come to the part of the project that instills fear in many a modeler—namely, water. I admit to having a certain amount of trepidation myself while progressing to this stage. Although by necessity the water work must wait until near the end, it still loomed large in my mind as I wrestled with how best to achieve the effect, **4**.

Many modelers use a resin of some sort and pour the mixture over a sealed, painted surface. However, this can be messy, and I preferred a simpler solution. I ultimately decided to apply layers of gloss Mod Podge over a painted tempered hardboard surface after viewing a video of Dave Frary demonstrating the approach. The hardboard (Masonite is one brand name) provides a flat surface for the paint and does not have the surface irregularities or the warp of plywood.

5 The plywood harbor has been removed to use as a template for the tempered hardboard that will be the base of the harbor. I removed all the scenery and structures and temporarily laid them on the floor beneath the layout. I added wood spacer strips to the harbor support frame to bring the hardboard up to the proper level.

6 I painted the hardboard harbor surface and glued it into place.

7

Next, I glued the scenery and structures into place.

8

I began to add Mod Podge using a flat brush.

I removed the plywood harbor cutout and used it as a template for cutting the hardboard, **5**. The piece of hardboard was not quite large enough for the entire harbor and log pond, so I spliced a small section within the log pond to cover the whole area. I used a scrap piece of hardboard for the splice, gluing it directly under the harbor-log pond sections. I knew that I would be adding logs to the log pond to conceal the seam, so I didn't worry too much about it.

I painted the hardboard with acrylic craft paints, **6**. I started with a base coat of black, then dabbed primary blue into the black for the main portions of the harbor. I left the blue out of the paint directly under the wharf and dock to simulate shadows.

I dabbed some forest green into the black paint within the log pond to represent murky water. I also applied brown paint along the rocky beach area. I later repainted the waterways a bluer color and smoothed out the blotched effects.

The blotches looked reasonable by eye but when I took some snapshots, the resulting photos did not look realistic to me. This is an example of how using a camera can clue you in on what might be amiss in your modeling. I also softened the shadow effect below the wharf and repainted the log pond with a smoother coat of green-black paint.

Note that the dabbing method leaves brushstrokes, or impasto patterns, in the painted surface. This in itself provides an appearance of waves. The effect will become less pronounced as the Mod Podge is added.

Once the paint had dried, I glued the harbor in place. Because the hardboard is only ⅛-inch thick, I needed some ⅜-inch-thick spacers on the benchwork supports to bring the water level up to where the banks had been modeled. To make the spacers, I asked a friend to rip ⅜-inch-thick pieces from 1 x 2 pine. I glued these pieces to the benchwork, then glued the hardboard to the spacers with wood glue.

With the harbor in place, I affixed the banks, bridge abutments, retaining walls, and pilings using Aileen's Tacky glue, **7**. I sprinkled talus, dirt and small plaster rocks along the beach and affixed them with diluted white glue. Before adding the wharf and dock, I applied a thick coat of Mod Podge to the harbor under these models and pushed them into place. I then proceeded to add Mod Podge throughout the rest of the harbor, **8-10**.

I first used a flat brush, applying the Mod Podge carefully along the banks, retaining walls and pilings, then filled in the remaining areas. After coating the area with the flat brush, I pressed down on the Mod Podge with a soft round brush to create wavelike patterns. It's a bit tricky to add the Mod Podge under the wharf, but if you proceed systematically you can build up the layers effectively.

I applied four coats in this manner to simulate depth on the wavelets.

Tapping down on the Mod Podge using a round brush simulates waves.

The first layer of Mod Podge is complete on most of the harbor. The Mod Podge will become clear as it dries.

The final detailing of the rocky bank shows white water crashing against the shore and the rear of Hooper's Oysters, including stilt supports and an oyster barge.

11

This sequence shows the model work after the water is completed.

Details may be added to the banks even after the water is completed. I glued small sections of fine leaf foliage to the banks using Aileen's Tacky glue.

The foam makes it easy to insert foundation posts for structures. I just poked holes where the posts will go and pressed the posts into the foam.

12

The sawmill is in place. More details will come later.

I followed this up with another application where I tapped in lines of Mod Podge with a flat brush to simulate taller waves approaching the rocky shore. I drybrushed Reefer White into this area to simulate air being entrained in the waves. Anywhere water churns, such as breaking on the shore or rocks, or in the wakes of boats, such "white" water will appear.

I did not glue down the Hooper's Oyster house, as I wanted to be able to remove this model for photographs. Instead I simply let the support pilings rest on the surface of the beach and the water, **11**. You can't tell the pilings are on top unless you look closely.

Further detailing of the retaining walls, pilings and banks can be done after the Mod Podge is completely dry, **12**. You can always add a little more in the future if you want to seat boats or other materials along the banks. I painted the bottom ⅛-inch or so of the harbor banks, retaining walls and pilings with Pavement craft paint to simulate a water-stained or eroded shore line.

The visual appearance of the water is strongly dependent on the lighting. When at least some of the light is in the forward direction (i.e., coming at you across the water) the water texture is highlighted best and the color also looks good. If the light is mainly backlit, the water appears flat and you can see the occlusions in the Mod Podge, which creates a dirtier appearance. I found that if you position a few strong lights around the layout aiming upward at the ceiling, the "bounced" lighting creates a nice overall look to the water.

Now that I've made at least one full pass through the layout, developing the scenery and structures, I can continue adding details to fill out the scenes. In the next chapter, I'll show how I operate this little railroad in a way that makes it feel like a much larger railroad system.

CHAPTER SEVEN

Finishing and operating

The layout is now largely finished. Further scenic applications—including grasses, shrubs and trees—can be added at my leisure, as can additional details, including vehicles and figures. Even a layout as small as this can absorb plenty of figures and details. For example, I placed a hiker sitting at the edge of the mountain lookout path overlooking Fort Bragg, **1**; this small detail catches most people's eye when they view the layout from this side.

A brave hiker sits at the edge of a lookout and waves at a train passing below. Details like this enhance a layout—creating mini-scenes and providing viewers with plenty of visual interest.

There are two choices with regard to figures: painted or unpainted. The latter are much cheaper, but you have to spend time painting them. I have a mix of both on my layout. For some figures, I've inserted a small wire through the foot and leg, which allows them to be "planted" in foam areas, keeping them upright. Others can stand by themselves on flat areas or sit on benches, etc. I generally avoid gluing them down so I can use them in different places, as need be, for photos.

Adding details and figures to the scenes is an enjoyable, ongoing process, **2**. All the structures—pier, boathouse, **3**, sawmill, etc.—can support them, as can the log loading area at Northspur. You can also invent mini-scenes of your own. You might include a camping party in Northspur, **4**, or picnickers near the Tiburon tower. Small boats can be added to the boathouse dock and other areas in the harbor.

Operations

Of course, another thing you can do as you are finishing up the layout is operate it. This is probably the most rewarding part of all—running trains through your scenery and switching the towns you've created. Personally, I like realistic operation, but I don't want it to be too

2

A brewery worker enjoys a break by the apple trees. A bench, figure and a few trees are all that's needed to set this scene. Every layout can support many such simple scenes.

complicated. I like to have a reasonable roster of cars that work well and a scheme that deploys them enjoyably.

The first order of business is acquiring the cars and engines. You don't need many for this layout; I get plenty of operating potential with a dozen cars—four boxcars, four flatcars, a hopper, gondola, tank car and reefer—along with one engine and caboose. I already had most of the cars from another switching layout I had built previously. For the new cars, I focused on models that would be appropriate for northern California: Southern Pacific boxcars, caboose and engine, and Canadian Pacific flat cars. Because of the layout's tight curves, you should stick with cars no longer than about 40 scale feet. Similarly, you should buy short engines; I selected a Broadway Limited Imports (BLI) Electro-Motive Division (EMD) SW1500 and have had no troubles negotiating the track.

3 Figures liven up the scene at King's Boathouse as a lone tank car sits at Bret's Brewery In Petaluma.

4

A pair of canoers pulls away from Hooper's Oysters while two other folks establish a camp in the right background. Both sets of figures and accessories are from Woodland Scenics.

5 I prefer to weather my rolling stock with paints rather than pastels because the cars are subject to handling. These Intermountain Canadian Pacific flat cars show new (top) and weathered (bottom) finishes.

How does it look?

You want your equipment to look good on the layout and operate well. Beyond the model itself, looking good is largely a matter of weathering. An easy yet effective way to weather rolling stock is to use craft paints in various colors and consistencies, **5-7**. I prefer weathering the rolling stock with paints rather than chalks because you will handle the rolling stock more often than structures or other scenic elements and the paint will not wear off.

I like to mix Territorial Beige and Burnt Umber to get a rust color, then apply dabs of paint to the trucks, wheels, and underbody, and a little on the couplers.

I then drybrush the car with a color like Warm Buff, taking care to apply the paint lightly in streaks straight down the sides. Additionally, for the flatcars, I used a hobby knife to deepen the grooves between deck boards, chip and scrape some of the boards, then I applied a black wash to darken the deck. A little Warm Buff can be added to simulate caked dirt and mud. I used beige, burnt umber, buff and black to drybrush the engine.

How does it run?

Looks aren't everything; the equipment also has to run well. The main mechanical issues I've experienced relate to the couplers. I want the cars to remain coupled as they pass over the magnets. It's tolerable if they don't always uncouple on the magnets, but it's unacceptable if they regularly uncouple when they shouldn't. This is more likely to happen with the last car of a train since there is no trailing weight to maintain tension in the couplers.

Sometimes a change of coupler is enough to make the difference. Many new cars have magnetic couplers, but they aren't always made by Kadee, and I feel Kadee operates best. Try replacing the couplers on failing cars with Kadee no. 148 "Whisker" type couplers. These couplers are easy to assemble and install.

If this doesn't work, you can add thin plastic strips under the wheel axles to provide resistance, held in place by the truck screws, **8**. Depending on the truck design, you may need to file the bolster near the screw to get a flat surface for the plastic strips. The added resistance is not an issue with respect to locomotive performance since the trains are short, five or six cars at most.

When uncoupling over the magnets, you may need to apply some manual assist if the cars don't automatically uncouple, or if the uncouplers don't open fully. This is easily accomplished by touching the metal "glad hands" that hang below the couplers with your finger or a small stick. You can use some sign or landmark next to the magnets to identify the magnet location.

To DCC or not to DCC?

During early stages of construction, I used an old direct-current (DC) locomotive, a Walthers Conrail SW1500, with a standard DC power

6 I use craft paints of various colors and consistencies to weather my freight cars like this Walthers Mainline Southern Pacific boxcar, new (top), and weathered (bottom).

pack. Later I purchased the BLI Digital Command Control (DCC) engine and ran it with an inexpensive MRC Prodigy Explorer DCC controller. I like the MRC controller; it is lightweight, compact and easy to program and use.

I have had more electrical issues with DCC compared to DC. Adding more feeders would probably help as DCC decoders are very sensitive to voltage levels. I've experienced more loss of power, both brief cut-outs and track discontinuities, and also had a major issue with static electric discharge completely discombobulating the engine. I was able to get it repaired under warranty.

When everything is running well, the DCC engine runs more smoothly at low speed and has a nice momentum effect. There are also realistic background sounds and other sound effects that can be activated by pressing the appropriate buttons.

I blow the whistle when crossing the road near the brewery, ring the

7 I like to mix Territorial Beige and Burnt Umber to get a rust color, then paint the trucks, wheels, underbody and a little on the couplers. This BLI Southern Pacific SW1500 engine shows the contrast between new (top), and weathered (bottom).

bell when backing up on the wharf, and apply the uncoupling sound effect when leaving cars at the sidings. I particularly like the uncoupling effect.

On a small layout like this, one pair of wires is sufficient for either DC or DCC, especially if the rail

joints are soldered. Powering the frogs would improve performance over the turnouts, but would add complexity.

Switching the industries
Most of the spurs accept a variety of cars and have loading spots for

particular car types, **9**. The sawmill spur accepts boxcars for loading lumber, hopper cars for receiving wood chips, **10** and flat cars carrying logs.

At Northspur, flat cars are spotted under the McGiffert loader near the rear of the spur and the gondola is

8 To improve coupler performance over magnetic uncouplers, I added small plastic strips to the trucks to increase rolling resistance. This keeps the train stretched out and the couplers engaged.

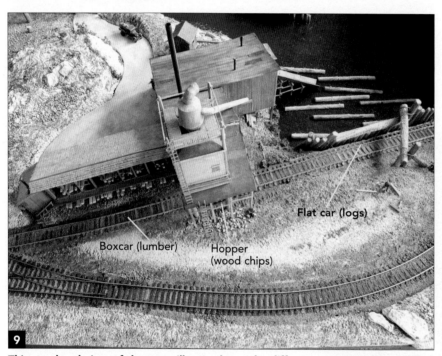

9 This overhead view of the sawmill spur shows the different car spots. From left, boxcars are loaded at the lumber shed, hoppers receive wood chips under the cyclone, and flats are unloaded at the poke.

Boxcar (lumber)   Hopper (wood chips)   Flat car (logs)

10 Engine 2476 has positioned the empty hopper to receive wood chips and is collecting empty flat cars for the return trip east at the Fort Bragg mill.

unloaded at the small dock up front. The Petaluma brewery accepts boxcars, reefers and tank cars; the tank cars are spotted at the rear of the spur where the unloading piping is "maintained."

The specific car spots add to operations, as the operators must decide how to best switch cars into the train as well as at the spurs. One last tidbit: engines are not allowed on the pier, so

an idler car is necessary to spot a car under the unloading crane. Flat cars are especially good for this purpose, **11**.

Flat cars are also used to carry logs between Northspur and Fort Bragg, from loading zone to sawmill and back. I manually position log "loads" onto the cars at Northspur and remove them at Fort Bragg, **12**.

More precisely, due to the nature of

the spurs—both the McGiffert loader and poke unloader have very tight clearances—I push one empty car of a pair of flat cars under the McGiffert loader, then place the load on the second car upstream of the loader. This arrangement indicates the cars being loaded. To remove the loaded cars, I pull the cars and place the second load on the empty car before leaving the spur.

This procedure is reversed at the Fort Bragg poke; I remove the load on the first car before it is pushed under the poke and leave the second car loaded until later when it is time to pull the empty cars.

I have other removable loads as well: a wood chip pile that can be placed into the hopper car and piping or equipment that can be placed into the gondola.

Operating with a crew

Operating the layout by myself is fun—operating with others is even more so. The three available operating positions are engineer, conductor and dispatcher. With two operators, one would run the train as engineer, and the other would keep track of train location (dispatcher) and issue switching orders (conductor). With three operators, all three positions are assigned individually.

The three operators position themselves around the layout. I attached small shelves made of tempered hardboard to the sides of the layout to provide supports for the MRC controller, **13**; this is where the engineer stands. The conductor stands on the opposite side, directing the engineer and attending to turnouts and uncoupling. I also added a small dispatcher's panel at the end of the layout, near the mountain, **14**. This panel contains a simple schematic of the railroad and allows the dispatcher to keep track of the train location.

Each circuit of the loop counts as one increment on the dispatcher panel. There are two increments between each town on the panel; therefore, the

A southbound train rounds a bend through a rocky cut as it pulls into Tiburon. Per the conductor's orders, two flat cars in this train will be exchanged for loaded boxcars, then the train will return north to Willits.

train will make two circuits before stopping and working each town. Clockwise represents trains traveling south and counterclockwise represents westbound trains. The dispatcher lets the engineer and conductor know when the train is approaching each town as progress is tracked on the panel.

At slow cruising speed, it takes a full minute or more to traverse the mainline loop. A complete out-and-back run from station to station takes about half an hour. Take your time and enjoy running along the main line and switching the various towns.

I've provided some examples of the train orders for a pair of Fort Bragg and Tiburon turns on page 95. I created these with plausible traffic patterns based on industry need. You can have fun inventing your own orders.

Note that the towns featuring trailing spurs require less time to switch since no runaround move is required. You may also decide that only trailing spurs are switched, so one set of industries is switched on the way out, and the other on the return. Many prototypes operate this way.

The train orders may be printed on paper and cut out to form individual instructions. They are then handed to the conductor when the train is ready to leave the station. Of course, the dispatcher should ensure that all the cars referenced by the order are in the correct locations to allow the orders to be fulfilled.

The station track can hold three cars. By extending it another foot or so (using a small detachable platform), two more cars may be added. The dispatcher places the cars by hand, then the train departs either westbound or eastbound. While the train is away and operating on other parts of the layout, more cars can be added to the station track to prepare for the next train. When the first train returns to the station, the cars are exchanged.

More extensive additions can also be added to the station track. A small yard is one example for those who would like to make up their trains

12 I remove the load from first car before pushing the cars into the Fort Bragg spur.

13 A simple shelf made from tempered hardboard holds the MRC DCC controller.

14

This simple dispatcher's panel keeps track of operation with a schematic and a locator. At this moment, an eastbound train is midway between Fort Bragg and Northspur.

hands-free. I have an old 2 x 4-foot switching module that can be attached to the station track; this module represents a small town with three industries and a short passing track, **15**. (For more on the Town of Hamlin layout, see the September 2016 issue of *Model Railroader* magazine.)

A dedicated DC-powered switcher takes the cars from the station track and delivers them to the industries while placing the cars from the industries on the station track.

For this to work, the station track must be electrically isolated from the main Northspur wiring and a switch used to direct control to either the Northspur engine or the engine on the switching module. Make sure the DC engine is isolated before switching the yard to DCC to avoid damage to the motor. Also, ensure the DC power can't feed back to the DCC system through a pair of metal wheels across the gap. You can never have too many switches!

Finishing the layout

I painted the layout edges dark green to help frame the whole scene. I added

15

a 2 x 4-foot backdrop behind the Noyo Canyon scene; I happened to have this backdrop from a previous module. I made the backdrop from a piece of tempered hardboard painted blue, with white cumulous clouds painted here and there, and the Tall Timber scene from the Walthers Instant Horizons line cut out and pasted on.

I painted a continuation of the water below the bridge onto the backdrop to better blend the scene. I position the layout so the backdrop rests against a wall with room along the other three sides for operators to stand. You can also add skirting below the layout for a more finished appearance and to hide items you might want to store under the layout.

I hope you enjoyed the story of the Northspur & Tiburon railroad. I thoroughly enjoyed building it and continue to have fun operating it. I want to acknowledge the modelers who captured my imagination when I was boy and who ultimately inspired me to build this layout: John Olson, Malcolm Furlow, Dave Frary and John Allen. And last but not least, my father who started me out in N scale.

Train order
Fort Bragg Turn No. 1

Arrival (actual minutes)	Departure (actual minutes)			
	0	Willits	C B1 G E	Depart westbound with loaded gondola for Northspur and empty boxcar for Fort Bragg
3	7	Northspur	C B1 F2 F1 E G	Drop gondola, pick up two loaded flat cars
10	17	Fort Bragg	B1 F2 F1 E B2 F4 F3 C	Drop boxcar and two loaded flat cars, pick up loaded boxcar and two empty flats, reposition engine and caboose for return trip eastbound
20	30	Northspur	F4 F3 G E B2 C	Drop two empty flat cars, reposition gondola
33		Willits	E B2 C	Return with loaded boxcar

Train order
Tiburon Turn No. 1

B – Boxcar   G – Gondola
C – Caboose R – Reefer
E – Engine   T – Tank car
F – Flat car

Arrival (actual minutes)	Departure (actual minutes)			
	0	Willits	E B2 R C	Depart southbound with empty reefer for Petaluma and loaded boxcar for Tiburon
3	6	Petaluma	E B2 C T R	Drop empty reefer, leave tank car in place
9	16	Tiburon	B2 C B3 B4 E	Drop loaded boxcar, pick up two empty boxcars, reposition engine and caboose for return trip northbound
19	27	Petaluma	R B3 C T B4 E	Drop empty boxcar, pick up empty tank car
30		Willits	C T B4 E	Return with empty boxcar and tank car

I built the Hamlin module several years ago. Adding it to the N&T layout expands operations.

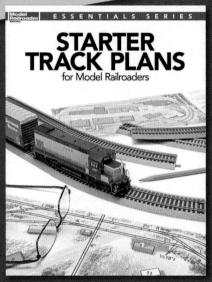
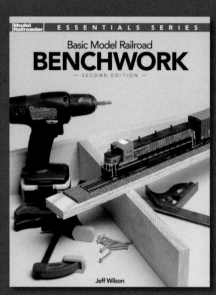
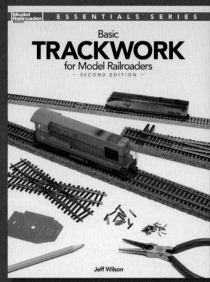
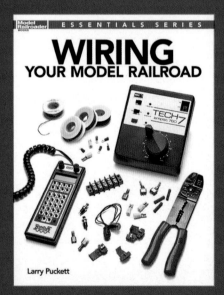